MADHOUSE

A 20 Year Retrospective

JONATHAN KIDDRANE

© SCHWABBOOKS

<u>*Madhouse:*</u>

a mental institution.

a psychiatric hospital.

a scene of extreme confusion or uproar.

<u>Stark Raving Mad:</u>

completely crazy.

<u>*Bat shit crazy:*</u>

A person who is bat shit crazy is certifiably nuts. The phrase has origins in the old fashioned term "bats in the belfry." Old churches had a structure at the top called a belfry, which housed the bells. Bats are extremely sensitive to sound and would never inhabit a belfry of an active church where the bell was rung frequently. Occasionally, when a church was abandoned and many years passed without the bell being rung, bats would eventually come and inhabit the belfry. So, when somebody said that an individual had "bats in the belfry" it meant that there was "nothing going on upstairs" (as in that person's brain). To be BATSHIT CRAZY is to take this even a step further. A person who is bat shit crazy is so nuts that not only is their belfry full of bats, but so many bats have been there for so long that the belfry is coated in bat shit. Hence, the craziest of crazy people are BAT SHIT CRAZY.

Authors Note

A first edition of this book was released prior to the outbreak of the Coronavirus. The stipulations made throughout this book address the many ways I feel our world has gone completely insane. With the addition of the Coronavirus to add insult to injury, this book takes on a somewhat austere quality. I could not have imagined our world becoming victim to such a thing.

When reading this book now, I am at a loss to fully comprehend how more crazy everything could become. I ask you the reader to keep this in mind when reading my thoughts and comments related to a pre-virus existence here in America.

The madness related to hearing entire countries have been placed in lockdown; complete with curfews and endless stories of a rising deaths in every nation does not begin to explain the insanity. Still, despite these experiences, the madness ensues. The most astounding nature of what this global crisis represents, is the continuing basis of this books intention; more people are crazy in ways we will never truly comprehend.

The one group in our society who cannot be placed in any category of normal human behavior is the rich. With the spotlight elsewhere, on a world-wide pandemic; the actions of the rich and famous prove how removed these people are from the world at large.

It needs to be documented how removed these people are from the world, or I suspect they will again regain their populace hold on our society.

Sadly, I believe there is nothing in place to stop the elite members of society from sharing their narcissistic disease. Stories of how clueless some members of society act during a worldwide epidemic is disheartening. During the first days of the virus, videos appeared on-line of multiple celebrities singing the song "Imagine" by John Lennon. Seriously? The banality of such performances further displayed the separateness these individuals have from the everyday person.

Celebrities telling people to stay home and listen to the authorities is further proof of their ignorance. Most of these people have homes that are the size of city blocks. Some of them have indoor and outdoor pools. Many have enough square footage to avoid family members for days if not weeks. The irony of such acts of privilege is astounding.

Other acts of pure ignorance come from the ways our elected officials use the crisis for political gains. All in all, it needs to be mentioned, despite all the rhetoric that will happen when this cloud over the world dissipates, our world leaders reacted in ways that require our appreciation. There will never be any formula in place for handling a pandemic. Despite all the precautions, a virus of powerful proportions, will always have an upper hand related to how it can wreak havoc on the world population.

If anything, when all is over and solved, continued efforts must be adhered to better control future outbreaks. These efforts require world leaders to put aside their pettiness related to controlling oil consumption, food distribution and the curtailment of pollution throughout the world.

The inept local leaders in different cities and states, in my opinion, should be removed immediately from their positions. There should be recognition by all, that during a crisis of epic proportions, idiots in positions of authority should be removed from their jobs. They need to be treated like captains on ships where the crews exercise their right to mutiny.

The restrictions placed on society for reasons of keeping us healthy should require a recognizable and embraced rule book. When working for corporations, throughout my career in telecommunications; I was tasked with writing disaster recovery plans. Every plan included requirements I recommended needed to be put in place to avoid disasters.

When presented to management at these corporations, the suggestions were always met with disagreements. The recommendations required the purchase of back-up systems to avoid problems in the event of fires, flooding, earthquakes, electrical outages and any other feasible disruption to daily working conditions. The meetings to discuss these plans brought about one of the first indications I experienced related to how stupid people can be.

It amuses me now, to comprehend that these same men and women who sat in positions of power in the corporations I worked at put so much emphasis on a hoax. I was tasked with ensuring the computers systems worked after something called the Y2K crisis. I ensured these people, nothing would change. They would not believe me. Instead, they budgeted millions of dollars to bring in computer experts. In retrospect, the Y2K crisis as it was called, brought to light how gullible and ridiculous members of our society can be.

I can only surmise what kind of disaster recovery plans are being written today to address situations that cause entire industries to close their doors. If I were still working in these companies today, I would recommend that every company have in place at the minimum, a year's salary for all of their employees. This kind of suggestion, despite the events related to a pandemic would most likely be considered unwarranted.

In our modern world, the bottom line is always the most protected asset of any company. The bogus claims related to respecting and appreciating the work force, in my opinion, is the first casualty of war. When and if you dear reader find the time to read Madhouse, I suggest you realize the most valuable asset in our lifetime is the sanctity of family.

During the Coronavirus, the most susceptible to the disease were the elderly. The youth culture for the most part needed to reminded time and time again that they could not do the things they did on a daily basis. It is my belief, that years of instant gratification distorted their understanding of life's real needs. They suffer from a far reaching disease, not yet registered with any health oriented study. The disease of having what they want when they want it. Sadly, it is not something that will change.

The madness will only get worse.

Prologue

In the 1968 film "The Planet of the Apes," starring Charlton Heston, Roddy McDowall and Kim Hunter, the impression is made about a future society gone completely mad. The depiction of a society where apes were rulers of the planet brought about a very interesting sci-fi movie empire. Four sequels were made and America embraced the concept of this imagined world. Remakes have scored much success through the years. Despite Hollywood's need for subsequent storylines, the original story was based on a 1963 novel written by Pierre Boulle. The ending in the book is not the same as the sensationalized ending in the film. In a scene whereby Heston as the main character Taylor, is shown in a jail cell being hosed down by one of his captors. He screams out, "It's a madhouse!"

My original idea for a title for this book was "Bat Shit Crazy." To avoid any comments about this title being too abstract, I thought about calling it "Stark Raving Mad." However, after deliberating on what I wish to share; the scene from this film fits into the insanity I see all around us. There are different ways of defining modern culture, however for the sake of clarity; and in an effort to be all inclusive – "Madhouse," in my opinion sums us up as a society perfectly.

In our modern world, knowledge is no longer a power. It seemingly in many ways distorts one's ability to think rationally and embrace any semblance of common sense.

> "Any fool can know. The point is to understand."
> **Albert Einstein**

What this book will attempt to share is how each person today, including myself, has very little understanding of our progress as a species – no less the ability to comprehend our differences and what make us unique to one another. The latest trends and beliefs associated with our differences are now being used to categorize us in ways that stagnate us from reaching higher levels of intelligence.

The one trend or interest best used to separate us in to demographics is the same trend most Americans today rely upon as a source of our daily information. Our reliance on technology has been slowly taking hold of our ability to think as rational human beings. There are many studies to substantiate this claim. The studies are most times conducted by the same Corporations we rely upon for our information. It is my belief any independent study, can be traced to Psychiatric organizations affiliated with colleges or state-run Departments of Health.

I will attempt to comprise logical examples of my claim that we are all nuts. This effort will most likely be the easiest part of this books research. On any given day here in America, our newspapers and news outlets prove the status of unrest and the insanity all around us. The writers of articles and the hosts of cable news stations themselves; border on compromising any means of intelligent discourse. In more ways than can be calculated, they, as news sharers, have become in many respects responsible for the ongoing decay of human intellect.

The other culprits responsible for our mental instabilities are viewed as entertainers. Late Night TV shows and their hosts manufacture a daily regimen of nonsensical attacks. These attacks, in recent years are aimed at making anyone not of their mindset and not subscribing to their political views as being unwelcomed, and more importantly painted as insane.

The biggest culprits of all, throughout the past several years are actors and singers. Many of these individuals, it is my opinion, male and female in these forms of entertainment, are no longer capable of acting no less worthy of being called singers. The crafts they are privileged to perform many times no longer relies on human talent.

Instead, with the advances of technology, most movies today are often special effect extravaganzas with actors thrown in to make the scenes more plot driven. Where upon singers, and music performers, are provided with enhancements in the studio that questions their actual abilities as artists.

These are blatant claims which I understand will not be received well. I will offer in my defense, my age. I am not a member of the youth oriented culture here in America. I do not subscribe to the same ideals younger generations embrace. This book is a testimonial that I offer to the society of which I am a member. If you disagree with my findings, with my opinions, with my views, I challenge you to write your own book.

Also, as an aside to this claim of our being BSC (Bat-Shit-Crazy), I will add to this essay driven tome; letters and articles I sent to local newspapers. Too often today, the concept of sharing our opinions and idealisms are lost to on-line commentaries. I do not subscribe to such modern meanderings. In my mind, anything published exclusively on-line is suspect.

One of the best displays of explaining the idiocy of politics came in 1870 from Mark Twain. It comes from a story he wrote for The Galaxy, an American monthly magazine founded in 1866.

The story "Running for Governor" detailed the humorous manner of how politicians are viewed to this day. Mark Twain, *was born **Samuel Langhorne Clemens** (November 30, 1835 – April 21, 1910), known by his <u>pen name</u> **Mark Twain**, was an American writer, <u>humorist</u>, entrepreneur, publisher, and lecturer. He was lauded as the "greatest humorist this country has produced", and <u>William Faulkner</u> called him "the father of <u>American literature</u>". His novels include <u>The Adventures of Tom Sawyer</u> (1876) and its sequel, the <u>Adventures of Huckleberry Finn</u> (1884), the latter often called "<u>The Great American Novel</u>". (Wikipedia)*

In this story, he told of his being asked to run for Governor of New York State as the candidate for the Independent ticket. Immediately after accepting the nomination, he was lambasted in local newspapers for perjury – with accusations claimed by 34 witnesses he robbed a helpless woman in Cochin, China. He had never been to Cochin, China.

Remaining silent, the newspapers picked up on the accusation and denigrated him for not responding to the charges. In another article, he was accused of robbing cabin-mates while visiting a Montana farm. He dismissed these claims by stating he had never been in Montana.

Other accusations were reported on a daily basis, until Mark Twain advised he was charged with burning a lunatic asylum with all its inmates because it obstructed the view from his house. After everything reported about him in the papers, he wrote – "I gave up. I hauled down my colors and surrendered. I was not equal to the requirements of a Gubernatorial campaign in the State of New York, and so I sent in my withdrawal from the candidacy."

The point being, the madness of being convicted by public opinion based entirely on hearsay and ridiculous accusations has been a mainstay of this country's makeup for as long as there have been newspapers and the now highly toxic social media society we live in.

Chapter 1

My Constitution

The following commentary did find its way in to print on the pages of a local newspaper. When posting the link for the article on my social media pages, I was amused to discover how many people misinterpreted my original, albeit sarcastic bent on explaining how I feel towards the political interpretations in place today. I am tired of how such interpretations appease a certain agenda. I wish to acknowledge from the outset of this book that I am not a registered Democrat or Republican. As a registered Independent voter – I feel there are often too many sides to any issue when it is argued for or against by someone affiliated with a single party mindset. This comical and much influenced piece of dogma by a favorite author, Kurt Vonnegut Jr. is an excellent jumping off point for this book.

> There is a tragic flaw in our precious Constitution,
> and I don't know what can be done to fix it.
> Only nut cases want to be President.
> Kurt Vonnegut

<u>*My Constitution*</u>

I woke up today and my Constitution was not the way it is supposed to be. I am wondering if it is something I ate for dinner last night. Maybe it's something I watched on TV? Or perhaps, it's something I read in a newspaper or on my computer? My Constitution has always been a reliable source of something that makes me feel secure in what I choose to do every day.

I think my Constitution is the same as yours. Surely, there's no other way to interpret what can cause such unrest. There's a lot of food for thought when it comes to how many different ways my Constitution can feel so upset. I used to be able to eat whatever I wanted. I used to be able to listen to everything with an open mind. I used to be able to read everything and not feel my Constitution being tied up in knots. I am wondering if this an age related ailment or if I have been poisoned by something or someone?

I fear this problem is only going to get worse in the next year. My Constitution cannot tolerate so many different interpretations and compromises. I keep searching for different remedies. I used to go to the movies and be entertained.

Now I have to worry if the movie will cause my Constitution to explode in anger or fear. I used to enjoy watching sports on television. Now I have to worry if my Constitution will be upset by something that's not a part of the game. I keep telling

myself my Constitution will solve its own problems. My
doctor says all of his patients suffer from the same problem.

He says there's no medical solution to how my Constitution is
feeling today. I wonder if my Constitution can discover its
own cure. I thought about taking a long walk.

But my Constitution cannot tolerate the different ways others
with the same disease carry on after being upset. I thought
about taking a long drive. But my Constitution cannot
understand why so many people are trying to get places faster
than their vehicles can get them there. I don't remember my
Constitution having so many different emotions. I don't
remember my Constitution being left open to such scrutiny. I
think the only way to solve this problem is to become an
astronaut. Maybe in outer space the gravity won't weigh my
Constitution down. Maybe on another planet my Constitution
won't feel so torn apart. I'm going to look into this possibility.
Now all I have to do is convince the people I love to follow my
lead. I wonder if they want to feel better too? Maybe they like
the way their constitution is making them feel? Maybe they
have stronger stomachs for these things? There's got to be an
explanation for this problem.

Perhaps I should try a different diet? It can't be healthy to
swallow the same dirt every day. If I can't become an
astronaut, maybe I should look in to joining a cult. They have
strict rules about thinking and feeling outside of the box.
When did the box become so confining? My Constitution may
need an overhaul. It cannot stand up under all of these
changes. Maybe I should stop watching TV? Maybe I should

stop reading? Maybe I should change my medications? My Doctor says he's giving a lot of his patients' lobotomies. He says once they have their brains removed, they feel a hundred percent better.

I asked him if I will be able to keep my good memories. He says it's a risk I'll have to take. I scheduled my lobotomy for November 2020. He's booked solid until then. In the meantime, he recommended I write everything I want to remember down in a journal.
He says, my Constitution will never be the same after I empty my brain. That makes a lot of sense to me.

The premise or intent for writing this piece had much to do with the different ways we hear both Democrats and Republicans interpreting the First Amendment today. The First Amendment of the Constitution of the United States reads as follows:

"Congress shall make no law respecting an establishment of religion, or prohibiting the free exercise thereof; or abridging the freedom of speech, or of the press; or the right of the people peaceably to assemble, and to petition the Government for a redress of grievances."

The constitution was adopted in to law in 1791. A law, which is over 225 years old, can in many ways be interpreted to suit the needs of any one relying on its meaning. When it is dissected by today's standards of living; there is a sudden clash of opinions related to what the amendment represents. If taken apart line by line, it is easy to understand how different definitions arise.

"Congress shall make no law respecting an establishment of religion..."

From the very outset of this statement, one can take issue with the provision that all faiths are being labeled equal. I personally take no issue with this right. However, there are individuals who exhibit emotions and opinions that their particular religion or belief system is better than another. To prove the insanity of a modern mindset toward this amendment, it is necessary to define the word religion:

- *The belief in and worship of a superhuman controlling power, especially a personal God or gods. A particular system of faith and worship. A pursuit or interest to which someone ascribes supreme importance.*

This is the first example of definitions that I found after typing *Define Religion* on my computer. By seeking a more broad explanation, WikiPedia defines religion as -- *a social-cultural system of designated behaviors and practices, morals, worldviews, texts, sanctified places, prophecies, ethics, or organizations, that relates humanity to supernatural, transcendental, or spiritual elements. However, there is no scholarly consensus over what precisely constitutes a religion.*

The definition goes on to say - *Different religions may or may not contain various elements ranging from the <u>divine</u>, <u>sacred things</u>, <u>faith</u>, a supernatural being or supernatural beings or "some sort of ultimate transcendence that will provide norms and power for the rest of life. Religious practices may include <u>rituals</u>, <u>sermons</u>, commemoration or veneration (of <u>deities</u>), <u>sacrifices</u>, <u>festivals</u>, <u>feasts</u>, <u>trances</u>, <u>initiations</u>, <u>funerary services</u>, <u>matrimonial services</u>, <u>meditation</u>, <u>prayer</u>, <u>music</u>, <u>art</u>, <u>dance</u>, <u>public service</u>, or other aspects of human <u>culture</u>.*

If there is any doubt, something written 225 years ago can be misinterpreted and argued in such ways as to make anyone appear totally mad? Our forefathers could not have envisioned a society 225 years into the future. The simplicity of the original statement related to religion constitutes a willingness to accept all people and their religious affiliations. Given the wanting nature that faith not be held against anyone, a deeper analysis of how time has evolved in to the many aspects of believing in God has changed, deserves a higher degree of clarification. It is crazy to assume this line of reasoning could anticipate the many different religions that are practiced today in America.

With this said, we must adhere to the more important line of reasoning declared by the amendment itself – Prior, to the declaration, the law stipulates – *"Congress shall make no law respecting the establishment,"* which to our forefather's credit, displays an understanding that <u>no religion</u> be held in such esteem as to be above the law.

The next line of the amendment specifies a further display of intended equality: *"Or prohibiting the free exercise thereof."*

And yet, our country is often divided when it comes to faith. What is faith?

Faith: *A complete trust or confidence in someone or something. A strong belief in God or in the doctrines of a religion, based on spiritual apprehension rather than proof. A system of religious belief. A strongly held belief or theory.*

The more we attempt to define religion and its subtext of faith, the more abstract any ability to fully understand what rights are actually being defended or opposed.

According to the online blog – *Christianity Today* – published in April 2018:

Even in an era where more of the nation doesn't ascribe to a higher power at all (10%) or believes in some sort of higher power or spiritual force (33%), a slim majority of Americans (56%) still believe in God "as described in the Bible," according to the Pew report.

This information has been updated in recent months to define less people today believe in God than these statistics share. In keeping with the premise of this book's title and my declared theory that we are stark raving mad, I pose the following questions:

- Why are we at one another's throats over something as abstract as religion or faith?
- What difference does it make whether a person believes in a God defined in a book of an

established religion or wants to believe in
something else?
* Who are we to say what is the best way to
exhibit faith?

These questions and the many more I could propose are only
the tip of the iceberg when attempting to understand how
insane it is to argue, no less believe, anyone has the inside
track related to God.

The amendment continues with its declaration as follows:

"…or abridging the freedom of speech"

It is quite easy to understand how such a respected right
should be embraced for all people always. However, what if
"speech" becomes propaganda? What if people in our modern
world subscribe only to those speeches they want to hear? Is
"speech" then respected as a right or does it become
something entirely different? Most recently in America, on
college campuses across the land, individuals have been
lambasted, ridiculed and physically harmed when wishing to
speak. They have been singled out as being unwanted for
merely having a different opinion than any given college
wishes to recognize as valid and respected. Herein, is where
the thought process of our idealisms become sadly warped. I
question how any person living in America today can justify
the actions of students who get away with censoring someone
wanting to share their opinions. It is indeed bat shit crazy to
believe or imagine anyone today should be afraid to voice
what they believe in.

I personally, must share my condemnation related to college students thinking they can be justified when displaying hatred toward a fellow student who does not see or believe things their way.

Furthermore, I think it is ridiculous to imagine so many young people saying they want to live in a world full of peace and love. And yet, they act like out of control mobs and uneducated morons when it comes to hearing opposing viewpoints.

As a young man, I joined the Army in pursuit of a degree in journalism. Life got in the way of the next rung in the ladder while in the military. My father died. Suddenly, I found myself wanting to be closer to home. The decision afforded me an opportunity which I can now safely say, put me on a different path for better things. Not a day goes by today that I do not thank God I never became a journalist.

When I was a young man, I believed journalist were the highest form of intelligence and most respected way of describing what happened. I wanted to pursue the events that shaped the world I lived in. I wanted to write about the ways people lived their lives every day.

Luckily, I was introduced to the world of computers long before they became the devices and instruments we take for granted today. I consider it a lucky break to have been at the forefront of computer networking. I can recall prototypes for electronic mail.

I remember how the advent of such applications revolutionized the corporations where I worked after getting out of the military.

I also recall how such applications as simple as e-mail changed the work place, in my opinion for the worse. Management no longer adhered to communicating with their staffs on a personal level. The mandate for sharing information became a process instead of an actual discussion of ideas and recognized achievements.

Modernization does not always move a society forward. The press today, made up of newspapers, magazines, and the latest movements toward total access to news on line; is by far the best example I can give related to our having gone bat shit crazy. Every individual subscribing to their own agendas and news source is akin to belonging to a group or gang that abides by their own set of rules.

A person who follows one news source eventually embraces the storyline or mindset of that paper, magazine or channel.

It can be labeled a modern form of brainwashing? A kind of brainwashing that everyone enjoys because it affords them to believe what they want to about everyone, everything everywhere. A kind of madness that their lives are in total alignment with the world around them.

The press today, is the comic book of yesterday. Super heroes and bad guys are displayed with an air for hero worship. I do not believe the respectability of the press will ever again be seen as worthy of any truth.

Unless, of course, the articles are about something outside the realm of absolute reality. Then the press can flex its muscles in ways that provide the grandiose ways to describe a new diet. Lest we forget the very high importance of a new fashion idea!

Dare we diminish the high praise and immense values of buying a new car or phone! The press then must be respected without question!

However, when it comes to politics, the press should be held accountable for inciting riots.

The press and media it rides upon should be placed in contempt for how each publication deliberately twists the truth to play in to their daily tongue and cheek narratives. Yes, the First Amendment protects these sad excuses for writing and display of false storylines. They have every right under the amendment to dig in to and tear at the fabric of truth.

"...or the right of the people peaceably to assemble,"

And assemble they do. The naysayers gather in the streets like mobs ready to attack anyone who doesn't embrace their way of seeing things. While in the Army, I came home on leave my first year and landed at La Guardia Airport in New York. A young woman came up and spit on me because I was wearing my uniform. I stood there dumbfounded. It was 1973. For all intent and purpose the war in Vietnam was winding down.

The storyline which has become the accepted narrative from this era says the anti-war protests and demonstrations from the 1960s put an end to the war. I find this narrative to be amusing.

The woman was either still practicing her right to assemble and protest or she was left over from one of the 1960s demonstrations in search of some kind of hippie validation.

It's my opinion when a war of any kind, anywhere, stops being profitable or manageable, it's ended.

My cynicism or skepticism is not a popular viewpoint. I accept that. However, when I hear how certain aspects of history are being   re-written every day to appease a certain agenda; I know for sure I must be bat shit crazy or witnessing a whole lot of people who belong in an asylum.

"…and to petition the Government for a redress of grievances."

The final line of the First Amendment is a powerful declaration of checks and balances. Our forefather's placed in to law the willingness to accept responsibility for any of their wrong doings. The ways and means we as citizens can voice our dissatisfaction with our government today is astounding.

The different methods of displaying our dislike of someone or something can be found on a daily – if not hourly or instantaneous basis today.

The ease of which we can air our grievances is no longer a personal or group oriented act; it's a full time network of complaints and differences of opinion found on our phones and computers.

A 24-hour extravaganza complete with Ads to buy new shoes, t-shirts and a million other much needed items for your home and car. In between our bickering and carrying on we can play video games or watch an episode of a favorite show. Our grievances are no longer about actual issues or problems. Instead, they fall in to a new demographic whereby we either LIKE what we are reading and seeing or we can demand it be removed at the click of a button! I will end this chapter with a question for Alexa. The device welcomed into many American homes with such enthusiasm and praise for its accommodating nature.

"Alexa, what is the meaning of life?"

"The meaning of life depends on the life in question, 42 is a good approximation."

The answer comes from a sci-fi novel, "*The Hitchhiker's Guide to the Galaxy*" by Douglas Adams. There is no explanation offered by Alexa when giving this answer. The computerized voice / device also can be interpreted to answer in the negative when asking it about Donald Trump.

The above interchange with Alexa is rather amusing in more ways than can be mentioned. The question – *What is the meaning of life?* – when posed to a device with Artificial Intelligence often changes based on an algorithm or whimsical thought. It is safe to assume, something I told computer users for years when I managed networks at corporations: A computer is only as smart as the person using it. That we have computers now sharing their political opinions further denigrates the ability to seek out truth in America. Instead, here in this first chapter, whether you agree or disagree with my dissertation on our First Amendment, surely you must agree we have all gone slightly mad.

Chapter 2

The Second Amendment

In keeping with our constitution as the jumping off point for this missive, I want to venture into the arguments about the Second Amendment. This amendment has gotten a lot of air time and paper in recent years. It reads:

"A well-regulated Militia, being necessary to the security of a free State, the right of the people to keep and bear Arms, shall not be infringed."

The proclamation is simple to understand. However, given our modern era, and the many different ways individuals interpret everything; a definition is required to provide what something means on many levels.

"…a well-regulated Militia, being necessary to the security of a free State,"

This rather open-ended declaration or provision for support of an Army, or police presence, to maintain order is without question a valid need in every country. Our forefathers foresaw a time when unrest and disgruntlements would or could place our nation at risk. It is idealistic or for the sake of my argument, insane logic to imagine otherwise.

To further delve in to the concepts believed by some that we unravel this right; it is necessary to define the word – Utopian:

Utopian - *modeled on or aiming for a state in which everything is perfect; idealistic. An idealistic reformer.*

I shall visit this definition several times in this book. An underlying belief posed by many in our society that we as human beings can live and exist in total harmony brings about a need to label a vast majority of people as delusional. Of course, everyone wants to live in a free society. Every individual on the planet earth wants to enjoy the freedoms found in a free society. The acceptance or willingness to embrace every person's form of identity is, in and of itself a utopian concept. We cannot adhere to any belief that endorses such expressions as being fully understood.

For the better part of the 21st century, this belief, that all people be accepted and embraced, based on their religious affiliations, sexual identities and cultural differences has created a form of delusional behavior that borders on anarchy.

I personally believe, if someone has no intent to harm another person, they have every right to believe what they want to believe, and embrace any sexual identity they deem called upon to feel good about themselves. I also adhere to accepting without any prejudicial emotions that a person's heritage and cultural practices are something that which makes them feel complete.

The problem lies in the expanse today, that each person be made to feel their way is the only way. This brings to light one of the major problems in a free society. A sense of entitlement by any individual or group introduces a challenge. The challenge in this situation, poses a threat to any other individual or group of people feeling the same way about his / her sense of self preservation.

Here too, in our modern world, we have been challenged to accept the meanings of his and her in our society. The degrees by which this distinction have been confronted, in my opinion gives further credence to our being crazy.

No matter how we analyze or distinguish the gift of life when born; mankind cannot be born in any other way except that of being a male or female. I will stop now, to acknowledge the proliferation of a certain portion of society born today with different sexual orientations. This acknowledgement cannot be discussed without defining what makes each of us human. A broad and easily misunderstood definition declares a man as someone with a penis and a woman as someone with a vagina. A more concise definition declares us with certain genitalia at birth.

*The **genitalia** include internal and external structures. The female internal **genitalia** are the ovaries, Fallopian tubes, uterus,* *cervix, and vagina. The female external **genitalia** are the labia minora and majora (the vulva) and the clitoris. The male internal **genitalia** are the testes, epididymis, and vas deferens.*

Much has been written and discussed in recent years about the acknowledgement of individuals who identify as the opposite sex in our society. One of the first widespread issues taken by circumstance related to sexual identity came about when transsexuals were deemed unworthy for military service. Here again, the use of a single word, "unworthy" brought to light much of society's disdain.

It is my understanding that the real issue was not that of the individual in question to serve in the military; but more so the use of serving by someone defining themselves in such a way as to use the benefits provided by their service to get operations considered way too costly otherwise.

Yes, it can be labeled as my being crazy, by leaping into sexual identities when discussing our Second Amendment. I assure you I could not agree more.

I hope to ascertain a defense for my jumping off points in this book. Then again, would it make a bit of difference?

I will delve further in to this modern day phenomenon related to sexual identity later in this book. I ask that you the reader indulge me while I attempt to prove my original reason for writing this book. This will not be the first time nor the last time I will dive in to a deep well to explain my thoughts and ideas.

" …the right of the people to keep and bear Arms, shall not be infringed."

This portion of the Second Amendment is by and large one of the biggest issues discussed today. The adherence declares that every person be allowed to defend themselves. There is no distinction in the proclamation that gives a person the right to harm others without provocation. The arguments raised with regard to taking away guns or limiting the amount of guns a person wishes to own are based entirely on events outside the realm of the law; further indicating a semblance of a warped common sense.

Any indication proposed by a governing body to take away or limit a person's rights in any way denigrates the absolute embrace of a free society.
The problems that have placed this argument at the forefront of national debate stem from a much deeper issue which our society in many ways refuses to acknowledge.

I will step off the ledge in saying that violence invites violence. I will go deeper in to the well and say there is undoubtedly, a growth of unstable men and women today than ever before in our history. The issues related to mental instabilities can only begin to help define the increase in mass shootings and bombings in a civilized society.

When a governing body declares a weapon of any kind be removed from the shelves, that belief places the blame of mass shootings and unwarranted violence on the item itself.

The arguments related to any weapon being the cause or instrument of evil, ignores the main reasons a person would choose to perform acts of violence.

It is my understanding; any instrument can be used to perform an act of violence. The instrument itself, cannot be held accountable, nor can it be used without the intent of the person choosing to use it to do harm to others.
Here again, we must return to the utopian mindset which adheres to believing all the world is one huge happy family.

By refusing to recognize any individual's tendency toward violent behavior, we become victimized by our own ignorance. Such issues of individual behavior cannot be swept under a rug.

Also, it is necessary to put in to this analysis the influences put upon a free and open society. Never before in human history have we experienced the onslaught of information and opinion on such a grand scale. The manner in which information is handled and received puts each of us at risk. Any individual who is not capable of distinguishing this information may be tainted, becomes a victim to how it can be misconstrued.

Further in to the problem of controlling violent tendencies, we can discuss at length the levels of violence displayed today.

Whether it is a television program, the latest films or the propagation of violent discussions on line; the average person today if left to squander in their own miseries, can lose their first line of rational thought – which for all people is the ability to understand right from wrong.

This chapter and the discussion of the Second Amendment, does not need further proof defining my claim we are bat shit crazy. By accepting the alternative belief that removing something / anything from society will make it a better, safer and more secure place to live is irrational. This is a blatant and overly generalized statement. I will discuss the exceptions to the rule in the next chapter.

<u>The thing about smart people is that they seem like crazy people to dumb people.</u>
Stephen Hawking

Chapter 3

Drugs – Alcohol and Other Vices

Are you on drugs? This line of questioning has evolved in my lifetime. As a young man, the question was often posed when I said or did something another person considered unacceptable. I posed the question when I felt someone did something I thought was improper. This distinction is still used today for the same reasons by most people.

Age, brings about changes, that without our wanting to admit, requires us to rely on things we never thought possible. In short: a vast majority of men and women today rely on drugs to keep them healthy. The medical industry has been one of the most prolific and successful industries in human history. Since the advent of medical procedures to enhance and save lives; the use of drugs to curtail issues related to poor health has made us in to a society reliant on many substances.

In reality, the question "Are you on drugs?" for most people of a certain age today demands a positive response.
The issues related to the word itself, does not include this categorization. Instead, when we hear the word "drugs" we

are immediately aware of the dangers of excess and reliance by individuals of a different sort.

The negative aspects of taking drugs requires a level of understanding what makes a person in to an addict. Addiction has been a problem for mankind since the advent of any substance or drug which can change or alter our way of thinking and behaving. A further in depth definition of addiction from my understanding, includes the use of anything which puts our health at risk.

The absolute comparison of health and drugs cannot be denied. This does not stop society from declaring any substance in ways to appease one's addictions. The use of the phrase, "recreational drug" which is defined as: *a drug (such as **cocaine, marijuana, or methamphetamine**) used without medical justification for its psychoactive effects often in the belief that occasional use of such a substance is not habit-forming or addictive.*

Is it anything but bat shit crazy to believe something / anything we cater to for bodily reasons as relief or escape to have a justifiable purpose? Herein, begins the vicious cycle of trying to comprehend drug culture as being acceptable in any form. At the farthest rung of the ladder when discussing drugs, a more plausible and highly recognized factor related to drugs is the manner in which it can be profitable.

While addicts need drugs to feel better about themselves or made to feel desensitized to the world around them; there is someone making money to make that happen. The formula for stopping drugs in any culture is called a War. There has been a _**War**_ on drugs since I was born. The use of drugs has always been an issue in our society.

The Drug companies despite their wanting to appear like they care, in reality are, in my opinion, like children on Halloween. The increase usage of drugs effects their bottom line. These companies who manufacture drugs that become addictive to its users end up making people rich.
This form or type of drug is just the tip of the iceberg when attempting to describe a society that has gone mentally insane.

As a young man, I played ball in the park. Behind the fences on the ball field was a wooded area. On any given day while I attempted to chase a fly ball or aim for those same fences when at bat, there was an awareness of kids my own age taking drugs.
What kind of drugs could they get their hands on? If and when a ball was hit over the fence, it became a scary proposition to venture in to those woods. While seeking the ball, I would see the faces of people I knew and saw around the neighborhood with their noses flushed red. They were not embarrassed, I was. They were addicted to putting their faces in paper bags full of modelling glue. Their eyes bugged out of their heads and they spoke in a way that made me question they had the slightest clue who I was or who they were at that moment.

What made them want to do such a thing? Their addictions changed as we grew older. I witnessed several of them throughout my childhood taking and using drugs that provided for them better highs.
I heard of several who had died from their use of drugs. This did not stop the others from continuing to take drugs. In their minds, I can only assume they believed their friend who died took the drug a wrong way. The concept of him or her having taken too much of the drug never entered their minds. It was simply a case of a right and wrong way to indulge in their daily vices.

Many of those friends from my childhood are gone now. The use of the word "friend" here is totally subjective. I did not understand them and they did not understand me. And yet, I would consider them all to be good people. I could not with a clear conscience understand what made them do what they felt they had to do. Hence, the feeling we are insane when we attempt to fight addiction by stopping the use of drugs. Instead, I feel we should try to better understand why a person needs such a thing to feel better about themselves. Here again, is the insinuation of better understanding one another before we try to distinguish what is best for all of us.

Drug use of any kind is, in my opinion a cry for help. Whether it is used to enhance or offer escape for someone, it is undeniably a means to justify the world around any addict. This definition can be utilized to explain alcoholism or smoking as well.

Alcoholism is an area of addiction too many people are familiar with today. Alcoholism has become secondary to the rise of opioid addiction.

The variations that explain why anyone becomes reliant on any substance is a question for the ages.

It is arrogant and naïve for us to think we can understand what makes anyone in to an addict on any level. This does not stop governmental agencies and private organizations from spending millions, if not billions of dollars a year guaranteeing they have a solution. It is crazy to attempt rationalizing how so much is spent trying to stop people from wallowing in their own misery.

Chapter 4

Sharing is Caring

The further we dig in to my theory of proving we are bat shit crazy, the deeper we go into attempting to understand one another. I have already opened the biggest can of worms on our plates today when discussing the First and Second Amendments of our Constitution. Here too, it becomes necessary to define something that governs and provides our shared rights:

*The **Constitution of the United States** is the supreme law of the United States of America The Constitution, originally comprising seven articles, delineates the national frame of government. Its first three articles embody the doctrine of the separation of powers, whereby the federal government is divided into three branches: the legislative, consisting of the bicameral Congress (Article One); the executive, consisting of the president (Article Two); and the judicial, consisting of the Supreme Court and other federal courts (Article Three). Articles Four, Five and Six embody concepts of federalism, describing the rights and responsibilities of state governments, the states in relationship to the federal government, and the shared process of constitutional amendment. Article Seven establishes the procedure subsequently* *used by the thirteen States to ratify it. It is regarded as the oldest written and codified national constitution in force. (Wikipedia)*

Let's agree, this is the most accepted or highly sort after definition of our nation's rule of law.
Accepting this as fact; it has been in existence for over 225 years, something must be recognized as being good and acceptable to most Americans. These elements of providing each citizen a ways and means to live in a free society, have functioned and given each generation a sense of comfort and security since its inception.

Today, these guidelines of recognizable and acceptable laws are being put to a test. It is my belief; albeit crazy in context, many in our government are threatened by how things are worded, no less how they are interpreted in a modern society.

First and foremost, it is necessary to discuss the philosophies surrounding Big Government. The definition reads as follows:

big government - *government perceived as excessively interventionist and intruding into all aspects of the lives of its citizens.*

Is it my understanding or am I being totally off base in believing many in our society today would rather be told what to do than have their own freedom to choose how they live on a daily basis? This feeling is visible to me when so many embrace so vehemently any adherence or opposition to a political figure. By allowing oneself to become enamored of or in absolute disdain for a person, place or thing – the ability to accept one's own sense of thought and action is suspect.

If there is one way of administering my sense of political belief, I would rather error on the side of caution than embrace totally any administration's practices and beliefs. To further define this in layman's terms, I resort to another article I wrote published in a local paper.

<u>It is Always Temporary</u>

There is a growing controversy throughout Queens related to what's best for all residents in our many unique and different neighborhoods. Throughout the borough, on every street, our differences are becoming a widespread problem.

Despite our different races, cultural backgrounds, and religious affiliations, we are now faced with political choices as an ongoing factor in defining each individual.
In every neighborhood, on any street, this one defining idealism is separating communities and families alike.

My 100-year-old mother-in-law, who has seen this nation's struggles and accomplishments, put it this way: "It's always temporary." Her insights and viewpoints add a very different picture to our current divide across America.

She has lived through 18 separate Presidencies, from Woodrow Wilson (1913-1921) to Donald Trump today. Throughout the changes in our years of war, economic depression, technical and medical advances, one thing stands out in her mind: the embrace of different cultures and people.

It is from this viewpoint we as a nation must make our united stand. What is happening to the American landscape cannot continue. The proliferation of opinions supporting one political mindset against another is an attack on all people.

When newspapers, radio and TV stations endorse a one-sided viewpoint, they are no longer reporting the news. Instead, they are acting as an a propaganda tool for the side they champion.

Our vast history as a nation has seen the challenges of war, the sacrifice of famines and the heartbreak of destruction. The destruction brought about by terrorism has left us scarred and forever mindful of how vulnerable the freedoms we all enjoy are.

The destruction brought about by disasters has left us aware of how the delicate balance of our daily existence can be changed in a heartbeat.

The very last thing any of us need is a media machine imposing upon us a partisan viewpoint. Whether it is an article, a letter or a comic strip; every aspect of leaning toward one side of the aisle serves to distract rather than inform.

What is occurring in our nation's capital today is more so an embarrassment than any semblance of encouragement for one party being better than the other.

The daily circus of who hates who is a disgrace. We as a people *know better. For every challenge, we as a nation have endured, we most need to celebrate what we have survived.*

It is unacceptable to witness our leaders acting like schoolyard bullies. It is more embarrassing to see our nation's reporters and chroniclers of history joining the fray. Our future deserves better.

Despite the interpretations of our historical strife, we have risen to the challenge of endorsing righteousness over ignorance. Whether it is the stupidity of racism or the acceptability of personal sexual identities, religious choices or allegiances, we have displayed a willingness to embrace our differences.

These many differences cannot be catalogued or placed in any suitable demographic. We are above the mindset of any poll designed to endorse a secular opinion.

I have to take the wisdom of my mother-in-law's comment to heart. In a simple phrase, her years of witnessing and experiencing our countries changes demands recognition.

It asks us to realize the main focus of our daily struggles. It requires us to take every challenge with a grain of salt. It displays the wisdom of time being our most cherished asset.

It's Always Temporary. The grandstanding of one politician over that of another is a brief line of defense, like a sand castle left overnight at the mercy of waves on a shoreline.

What is evident and the most relevant aspect of our daily conversations is respect for one another. The news happens because life happens. There's no room for interpretation. Tell the people what occurred, we will decide how to accept or deny the truth.

As we proceed today, we will carry the burden of accepting our differences or perpetuating our divides. The lines are all drawn in the sands of time.

This article was in response to the still growing admonishment of the President and our American values. The more relevant question related to modern politics must address how deeply and passionately we as a society have embraced or dismissed elements related to the last four years of our lives?

Again, we must be all be crazy to not recognize something is happening of which we have never seen before.

In my mind, and again I am not supporting one political party over that of another – although I do suspect one of the current parties here in America is in dire need of a brain transplant; it quite literally boggles my mind that we cannot look at this in a more rationalized manner.

If allowed to indulge your sense of common sense for a moment, what exactly turned us against one another with such a great divide? Is it the fact that a non-politician rose to the ranks of President? Is it possible many in our society fell prey to one of the worst concepts for becoming President in our history?

I speak here about the notion a candidate placed her entire bid for becoming President on the delusion it was her time. This concept of it being someone's – no less anyone's time to become the leader of the free world is in my way of thinking, hysterical.

The reactions by a multitude of people in our society, no less the desperate acts by the Democratic Party since the election of Donald Trump is proof enough to substantiate the claim we have gone insane.

The end result, no matter how it pans out will undoubtedly put at risk any trust ever again in any elected official. The overall description that will best define this era of America, most times alluded to in liberal media as the Trump-Era, is akin to children in a schoolyard.

The red rubber ball being tossed in the air around all of us has been lost. Where did it go? Instead of trying to look for it, we are arguing constantly about where it went. We are at each other's throats trying to find it. We have individuals trying to replace it with a new blue ball.

Suddenly, we are allowing ourselves to worry more about the color of the ball than whether or not we can ever again remember how to play nice.

Chapter 5

History as a Stepping Stone

If it was possible to pinpoint when we lost our ability to think rationally, I put forth the notion we should trace our mass delusional behaviors to the invention of television. It is interesting to discover how long televisions have played a role in our society.

When seeking to define the definition of the word television – again utilizing the most used source of modern knowledge Wikipedia we find the following description:

The invention of the <u>television</u> was the work of many individuals in the late 19th and early 20th centuries. Individuals and corporations competed in various parts of the world to deliver a device that superseded previous technology. Many were compelled to capitalize on the invention and make profit, while some wanted to change the world through visual and audio communication technology.

So as to not test your patience, I will not go in to the actual history of when televisions were invented – but more so share when they became a part of our everyday culture.

1941: First television advertisements aired. The first official, paid television advertisement was broadcast in the United States on **July 1, 1941** over New York station WNBT (now WNBC) before a baseball game between the Brooklyn

Dodgers and Philadelphia Phillies. The announcement was for Bulova watches.

When researching the one invention that has changed our way of viewing the world around us, you may discover different dates as to when TV came in to vogue. As early as 1928, people who could afford devices known as early televisions could receive weather reports and farm reports delivered to their screens twice a day, three times a week.

The in-home all over America TV shows we know today did not become popular until the late 1940s. It is safe to assume, at the end of World War II in 1945, the advent of mass produced television was born.

Is it possible, the end of WWII can mark our last vestige of common sense in America? Was it then, after celebrating the end of a war that we were told put an end to tyranny – that we as a society began to lose sight of our shared freedoms and idealisms?

The early days of television was innocent enough. Broadcasted shows depicted a ways and means for people to sit together and see things they would never have been exposed to otherwise in their homes. Variety shows displayed singers and circus acts which entertained individuals across America who were never exposed to things considered Big City entertainment. Comedy shows brought about the first examples for creating a nation-wide sense of humor on subjects often considered taboo or not welcomed into many living rooms.

Despite the early years of nationwide televised shows, being at times questionable related to innuendos on topics not often talked about, no less seen; nothing truly challenged the nations intellect. The defining moment, in my opinion occurred when the nation was exposed to the first televised debate by Presidential candidates on September 26th, 1960.

It is at this particular moment in our history, that several issues related to our political divide became a part of the national stage. It is at this particular moment, when John F. Kennedy as the Democrat candidate stood opposite Richard Nixon, the Republican candidate that we as American's lost our minds.

It is said anyone listening to the debates on radio believed the debate was a draw, with many giving the semblance of victory to Nixon. However, the 70 million viewers who watched the debate on televised were easily won over by something not seen before in a political arena.

Kennedy displayed an appearance of charisma and poise while Nixon appeared sickly and winded. This first introduction for many American's when discussing the power of television brought about the election of Kennedy.

The very next relevant moment in the long line of televised events that shaped our national insanity came three years later in Dallas, Texas. On November 22nd, 1963, John F. Kennedy was assassinated while driving in a motorcade down a street filled with well wishes and onlookers.

The unexpected moment of violence brought live in to every living room ushered in an era of viewing the television as more than a device designed to educate and entertain.

It is at this precise moment, we as American's witnessed madness like never before.

The Live Coverage of Events since that moment has brought about a change in how we as human beings have been exposed to death, mayhem and catastrophes. The 1960s, brought the horrors of the Vietnam War in to our homes. The 1960s introduced us all to the different mind sets around the nation. Protests and demonstrations related to those against the war as well as displays associated with the Civil Rights movement created an air of chaos unlike the experiences of past generations.

Our reactions as a society were both horrifyingly freighting, and ridiculously representative of a growing portion of our nation who felt the world should and could live in harmony. The delusional nature of this mindset put in motion a notion that anything less than a utopia was disappointing.

If we could take a step back for a moment, there were defining moments at the end of the 1960s, that forever link us all as being capable to get along in a grand way. Woodstock, in August 1969 gave life to the ideal, we can celebrate life freely. The landing on the moon in July of 1969 afforded people to feel anything was possible.

This embrace was short lived. The Vietnam War spiraled out of control. On December 6th 1969, at the Altamont Speedway in Northern California, the Rolling Stones were headliners at a concert many believed would parallel the success of Woodstock.

The disruption of the concert which ended in violence, clouded the belief many still embraced about their utopian dreams. Hidden in many ways from the same delusional thoughts prior to Woodstock, was the brutal murder of Sharon Tate and four houseguests who were all brutally murdered by members of a cult headed by Charles Manson.

Also, the madness that gave birth to our mental instabilities included the assassinations in 1968 of Civil Rights Leader Martin Luther King and Robert F. Kennedy. The turbulent 60s, as they are often referred, forever changed how we live in America.

Television, has become a member of every family today. The different ways we can watch anything from sports, to movies and games has made the television in to the most powerful weapon on the planet.

Everybody gets so much information all day long that

they lose their common sense.

Gertrude Stein

Chapter 6

Information

When setting out to write this book, I was motivated by the daily onslaught of opposing opinions on many topics which confront Americans. I am often disappointed in how my fellow Americans ascertain and interpret the information we are privy to on a daily basis. In the late 1960s, one television series "The Prisoner" challenged the notion related to information being used as an instrument against society. The series stands as a testimonial to the world we now inherited. While the daily exchange of information is regarded as both healthy and detrimental to those of us who utilize it – a much more dangerous and diabolical application is in use today. The labeling of such a vehicle as being detrimental to our nation's well-being is considered by many to be a generalization. However, I put forth the theory that what we say and do with regard to our opinions and use of social media is not beneficial to the overall health of our future.

One aspect of this theory comes in the form of ongoing suspicions and condemnation of the current best known social media application – Facebook.

The U.S. Government has a multitude of officials who have taken the notion of Facebook's social entities as being a negative influence on the intellect of its users.

What is actually happening, in my opinion, is the belief by government officials who deem Facebook a threat, we as users do not have the ability to think for ourselves.

In an article I published in a local newspaper, I posed this threat as Americans being gullible idiots unable to make heads or tails of what we might read or are being exposed to.

<u>The Gullibility of Social Media</u>

Much has been written in recent months about the responsibility of social media giants like Facebook, Instagram and Twitter. It is disconcerting to imagine how much power is shared with regard to our daily opinions, rants, raves and everyday comments.

What has happened since the advent of shared information is quite fascinating, not to mention how overly representative each social media platform can influence its members. Essentially, the creators and owners of social media organizations are being called to task for allowing ads and fraudulent information to reach its members.

Sadly, this accusation is highly suspect. What it truly means is how easily members can be duped into believing things simply because it appears on their phones and computer screens. What it further insinuates is the average user of these sites cannot think for themselves.

All information is now defined as truth based on how many "likes" it receives. The newest form of global warfare is in the hands of each person married to their technical devices.

Each person becomes an accomplice in ways to further separate truth from fiction and reality from fantasy.

The phrase "fake news," a prominent saying for several years, does not just represent false information, but also defines the growing number of individuals who rally in protest for things they know very little about.

When demonstrators are more likely to use social media to promote causes they only understand with quips of data on their phones, it stands to reason many are more interested in being seen rather than actually wanting to make changes in a civil society.

The process will only worsen as we reach 2020 and the election season. Since the government is seeking to blame the messenger providers, we must all keep ourselves informed in ways that do not rely on rumors and hearsay.

We are an educated society, and we should seek information by weighing the facts. We should not placate the social media fashionista or subscribe to news outlets that do not provide fairness as a part of their guidelines.

It is estimated over three billion people worldwide are on some sort of social media platform. No one is editing the content we receive every day.

There's an effort to censor with regard to profanity, which sounds noble in principle, however being offended by how something is worded hardly places checks and balances on the accuracy or authenticity of what we read.

Fewer and fewer people around the world read opposing viewpoints on issues we all deem newsworthy and relevant to our daily lives.

Instead, each individual caters to having their understanding of any issue substantiated by who agrees with them.

A study of any group on Facebook will inevitably lead to negativity delivered by the same members of the group who want to promote solutions.

The term "Second Life" refers to a person having the ability to create an alternate personality on the Internet. Each person's "Second Life" could be blamed for promoting opinions and commentaries.

Each person must willingly take responsibility for their own extended personalities on the Internet. If we cannot fully adhere to the sacred values of information, we are doomed to undermine our own precious rights in a free society.

The questions related to this article poses a higher threat to our future. The outcome of the 2016 election carries a life changing red flag for every American. The ongoing actions of one political party to chase after the election of Donald Trump should open the eyes of any person interested in our country's future. From where I am sitting, I see a government more hell bent on maintaining controls over each person; rather than accepting change is inevitable.

The Freedom of Information Act

*The **Freedom of Information Act** (FOIA), is a federal law that requires the full or partial disclosure of previously unreleased information and documents controlled by the <u>United States government</u> upon request. The Act defines agency records subject to disclosure, outlines mandatory disclosure procedures, and defines nine exemptions to the statute. The Act was intended to make U.S. government agencies' functions more transparent so that the American public could more easily identify problems in government functioning and put pressure on <u>Congress</u>, agency officials, and the <u>President</u> to address them.*

While the public may be aware of <u>news organizations</u>' use of FOIA for reporting purposes, they make up less than 10% of all requests with businesses, law firms, and individuals all being more frequent users.

The Freedom of Information Act was placed in to law in 1946. Since its inception, it has been ratified and updated several times.

In no way, did the original intention expect to see information so easily shared and implemented on a daily basis as it is today.

The original intention was to hold the government to task. The current manner in which information is shared cannot in any shape, form or way manage how anything is disclosed.

Chapter 7

"Ok Boomer"

The phrase OK Boomer was given prominence in 2019 when members of the younger generation took issue with anything aimed at them by anyone older than them. They especially did not or do not appreciate members of a certain age complaining about how they live their lives.

Generation Names	Births Start	Births End	Youngest Age Today*	Oldest Age Today*
The Lost Generation The Generation of 1914	1890	1915	104	129
The Interbellum Generation	1901	1913	106	118
The Greatest Generation	1910	1924	95	109
The Silent Generation	1925	1945	74	94
Baby Boomer Generation	1946	1964	55	73
Generation X (Baby Bust)	1965	1979	40	54
Xennials	1975	1985	34	44
Millennials Generation Y, Gen Next	1980	1994	25	39
iGen / Gen Z	1995	2012	7	24
Gen Alpha	2013	2025	1	6

Throughout time, generations have been named in accordance with the time they became members of society. In an effort to be all inclusive, and albeit politically correct – *which is akin to chopping off a part of one's brain to accommodate a semblance of understanding one issue, and – or, one person at a time;* the best way to describe the current lambasting of one generation by another reeks of dismissiveness.

Our modern youth oriented culture, while more involved with the issues of today, and admittedly better informed than generations before them, lack the one personality trait which afforded older generations a way to grow in to responsible adults. This statement is; in and of itself, inflammatory on many levels. First and foremost, it displays the same disregard for what the younger generation feels is their right to say about the older generations.

Quite fascinating is how the use of one word has changed throughout time. The word that has lost it's national, and world-wide meaning is – Respect.

Today, the word "respect" is often used to issue a threat. The word has been adopted by mobs or gangs, who consider street credibility more valuable than that of earning someone's admiration.

It has become necessary for members of our society to feel they deserve respect. The problem being, as anyone should know, respect is earned. It should not be used as a device or vehicle which threatens harm if it is not properly given or displayed.

The dismissive nature of our modern generations, whereby one generation, disrespecting any form of authority – can be traced to the 1950s. There were always some examples of one level of society disagreeing with their parents or adults in general. The 1950s, brought about a new breed of disagreement. Teenagers, in general, were made aware of the antics they could exhibit with regard to embracing a different kind of freedom. These freedoms introduced to them a whole new form of expression.

Whether it was fashion, rock and roll, or the exposure to other forms of adult oriented pleasures – smoking, sex, drinking and drugs – never before had a generation taken to being such a disruptive force in America.

Today, the basis for the ways many younger generations feel they can express their dislike of society stems from what I will call – rewritten and embraced histories.

I will take this moment, to fully disclose, my conclusions are based on personal opinion. This opens me up to a shitload of comments, of which I will neither defend or bother to explain. Instead, I embrace the attitude of today's youths by saying – Ok Boomer.

Which by way of explaining the attitude at all, simply means, if you don't agree with what I say, I shouldn't care. This response without needing to fully define it; is for lack of a better definition – crazy.

For the sake of your amusement – this bit of information may serve to further delude this manic dissertation: I discovered the following information on-line:

In the summer of 1953, "Crazy Man, Crazy" became the first rock and roll song to be heard on national television in the

United States when it was used on the soundtrack of *Glory in the Flower*, an installment of the CBS anthology series, *Omnibus*. This live production featured James Dean and was a predecessor to his later *Rebel Without a Cause*.

Bill Haley and the Comets performed the song in the 1954 Universal International movie short *Roundup of Rhythm*, which was the motion picture debut of the band in a musical short directed by Will Cowan that featured a D.J. and his female guest introducing the Comets. This film is regarded as the first rock and roll movie feature predating *The Blackboard Jungle* (1955) and *Rock Around the Clock* (1956). The band also performed the song in the 1961 Mexican film *Besito a Papa* (1961) directed by José Díaz Morales made by Cinematográfica Filmex S.A. and released on September 14, 1961.

These kind of facts humor me, as much as I hope they humor you the reader. The word itself, "crazy" took on a transformation at this particular time in our history – declaring anything deemed unacceptable behavior by society as "super cool." Which predates the notion of a later use of this kind of opposite appeal – when Michael Jackson, in 1987, utilized a word in his song - "Bad" to represent the same sort of sensationalized embrace of behavior over acceptable forms of expression.

*"**Crazy**" originated in the 1570s and was defined as "diseased, sickly." The term soon was associated with a specific group of people, those who had mental illnesses. Closely tied with the word "insane", "crazy" became a slur for people who were outside of the societal norm of mental health.*

The premise of this chapter helps to further emphasize my original theory that we have gone bat shit crazy. The evolution of music as a force of nature upon our senses has and always will be a powerful source of influence on all people. What happens when this weapon becomes more than the music itself?

In recent years, music has evolved in many ways. Setting aside the different ways we can listen to music for a moment; a growing list of artist are given a hero type worship which affords them levels of influence on those who listen to their music. When music becomes a form of propaganda, over that of it being an enjoyable form of self-expression, it can become detrimental to society. Here again, a statement which cries out for explanation. The statement could easily be misconstrued as having been written by a curmudgeon. I accept this classification. I wear it with honor. Ok Boomer?

As easily as the current generation can dismiss their smart ass antics of labeling one kind of person over that of another; I argue my right to exhibit the same kind of behavior. Staying with the topic of dismissiveness in our modern culture, the manner in which we can say things before actually thinking about what we want to say, is another example that best explains we are not using our brains properly.

When speaking with members of the youth oriented culture, I am often amazed by how well versed they are when expressing themselves.

They are far better at believing what they are saying is true than I was at their age. The information they are privy to on

topics which I am certain I knew very little about at their age,
no less even cared about, is astonishing and noteworthy.

Truth

 the quality or state of being true.
 that which is true or in accordance with fact or reality.

 a fact or belief that is accepted as true.

In our modern world, defining what is true and false can
become a slippery slope.
Relying on our resources to assist when trying to understand
if something is True or False opens all of us to a form of
indoctrination. Throughout time, the sources of getting factual
information have changed. As discussed in the previous
chapter, information, at best today, is tainted.

When using the Internet to look-up something, anything – it is
astonishing to discover, on any issue – whether it be about a
person, place or thing; truth or facts are most times open to
discussion. The Internet, came in to vogue, as we know it
today, in the 1990s. Prior to its introduction into the society,
the Internet in its infancy was a military tool to exchange and
study the different ways the world interacted on the global
stage.

Today, the Internet is, by and large the most used universally
accepted form of seeking information available. Many of the
current generation of computer users, have never lived in a
world that did not include access to the Internet. On many
levels, this availability, given their age, is in part a

dependency; on par with past generations not having access to beer on Sunday, cigarettes or drugs.

Add to this phenomenon, the levels by which the youth culture today can use the powers of shared information to promote themselves, their antics and forms of what they deem to be their savviness of society and our issues.

The very first use of the phrase OK Boomer, was by a group of students in a mid-west high school. The creation of the phrase was used to denigrate the Boomer Generation for not understanding them. It was also put in to the mainstream of our culture by individuals who took to their word processors, computers and devices to expound on the different ways they view our society is failing. Be it the environmentalist, extremist utopians, or the often still crying about being sent to bed at 10 years of age writers – who all believe the boomers are the blame for all things bad on the planet today. How are they using the word "Bad" I wonder?

Chapter 8

The Blame Game

Anyone can play along. It's a universal game of your fault – my fault. In recent years, the Blame Game has become the best form of entertainment on the planet. Rather than attempt to understand how anything went wrong, is wrong or is getting worse; we as a society opt to rely on our ways of feeling we are right. The Blame Game puts forth the kudo – "I'm Right – and You Are Wrong." The basis for our feeling this way stems from one form of absolute truth, which has taken on epic proportions of divisiveness. The best use of explaining how the Blame Game is played stems from the belief "If You do not agree with me, I will never agree with you."

The ease by which someone can be blamed for something – anything, comes from an unlikely source. First and foremost is the growth of entitlement in our society. Everyone deserves a chance to better themselves. Everyone deserves to be free. Everyone is equal based on our race, religious beliefs and ethnicity. What we are not entitled to is the practice of belittling another person simply on the grounds that we do not agree with them.

This practice is in many ways, the foundation of our failures in the modern world. We cannot sustain any level of respect for one another, nor our nation since this entitlement has been used so freely and frequently.

The manner by which every facet of our society deems it to be entertaining or self-ingratiating to belittle others, whether they be public officials, co-workers or classmates is a form of oppression. It is also, without exception a poor display of one's character or personality traits. It makes anyone who uses such tactics appear stupid. I will elaborate on the all-encompassing nature of entitlement undoubtedly many times in this book.

This generalization has some means of being warranted. It is warranted when lies and deception are used to express how a person feels towards his / her oppressors. It is difficult to support a person placed in the uncomfortable position of lashing out verbally or otherwise at people against them. Can there be a double standard when it comes to common decency? Should not every person have the right to defend themselves against oppression? What exactly is oppression?

Oppression:

- prolonged cruel or unjust treatment or control.
- the state of being subject to unjust treatment or control.
- mental pressure or distress.

A conversation could be had between individuals who experienced absolute oppression today and those who embrace it as a means of not getting what they wanted in life. There are many people seriously oppressed around the world today. Those individuals do not have the things every

American has without exception. Here in America, to declare oneself oppressed because something – anything did not turn out as you wanted it to; is lunacy.

To adopt such a badge of honor upon your shoulders, simply because things did not turn out as planned is insulting to the millions of people around the world experiencing hardships we cannot fathom. By allowing our society to feel we are in any way living in conditions that require such concern – is beyond my comprehension.

And yet, this is what many in our youth culture are being told. This is what they are told to believe – based entirely on something we all know is related to power.

A further denigration supporting the use of a double standard in today's world – is the misuse of fame to pretend something bad happened to oneself. In 2019, an actor, Jussie Smollet claimed he was attacked by white supremacist wearing Trump supporter hats. The claim turned out to be a hoax. For several days, he and the act itself was front page news.

There is no apology which can provide an acceptable way of changing how much the hoax damaged society. Hate Crimes are a travesty of human behavior. There remains a portion of society who believe the incident took place as first reported. In reality, the failed actor feared being fired from the show he was on. In dire need of seeking notoriety, he hired two members of the cast in the same show to beat him up. Such acts should be called what they are, a Hate Crime of the kind happening in a lot of people's heads – based entirely on

media instilled hype. This occurs because members of society believe only what they want to. The power of suggestion maligns for many, the ability to understand reality.
The old adage when defining the corruption of power, '*Power corrupts; absolute power corrupts absolutely*' has for many years been the end all and be all definition when posed as a way to define someone or something unacceptable in a civilized society.

Today, what can be defined as corruption is open to interpretation. Currently, we are watching the unraveling of corruption on a world stage. The means by which it is being used has far reaching consequences. When words and acts can be twisted to mean one thing when they mean something entirely different; we are all at a loss for understanding what is happening in the world around us.

There are certain words in the English language that take on different meanings when used in any opposition based on power. The current words being bandied about in the political circus are easily misinterpreted and can often lead to disagreement. The disagreements come from a wide variety of sources. The use of the word and understanding what it means in the context it is being used can cause confusion and divide unlike any other words used today.

In layman's terms, I was always told, "sticks and stones can break my bones, but names will never hurt me."
Why was I taught this lesson if it is not true? Individuals today use name calling like rockets in a war zone. How

sensitive have we become, if being called something –
anything is like a bullet through our hearts?

One portion of our society can call one another certain names,
but someone outside of their group says it – and they are
being disrespectful. How can a word be weaponized in such a
way as to make it more powerful? There are ways to
understand this in layman's terms.

Just as words mentioned previously in this book – "crazy"
deemed as slang for "cool" in the 1950s and "Bad" used to
mean the same thing in the 1980s; some words take on
different meanings in how they are used and who uses them.

It is considered derogatory to call people names which do not
constitute a level of respect. And yet, if the same word is used
to illustrate the embrace of someone; it can be easily
misunderstood; no less confusing for many in society to
comprehend why something is so offensive.

In the same ways, words like globalism and nationalism can
separate entire groups of people who are not of the same
mindset to understand how they are being expressed.
Globalism:
*the operation or planning of economic and foreign policy on a global
basis.*
Nationalism: *identification with one's own nation and support for
its interests, especially to the exclusion or detriment of the interests
of other nations.*
It is very difficult to substantiate support for anything that
may have been explained to someone as a means to promote

peace around the world. It is further made difficult to have anyone take pride in his / her own country if they are told it demeans their wanting to embrace all people equally. In both of these definitions, a more telling level of corruption can be discussed.

In today's society, many embrace the notion that we can all live in harmony. Who doesn't want to believe world peace in our lifetime is possible?
It's a universal desire to want everyone to live in a world without violence and oppression. It's also a pipedream worthy of serious psychoanalysis. The world and it's many different cultures cannot attain harmony when we have so many differences of opinion on how to accomplish this utopian goal.

There's an old standby when we are all growing up, which I hope is still taught in schools around the world today – "Love one another as you would have them love you." This lesson is a powerful way of understanding how we all wish to be treated. It is also, sadly, a utopian concept. The ways and means by which we expect to be treated is by far the hardest lesson to understand. One of the main misnomers of modern history stems from the reasoning many today give for their beliefs or intentions.

Pacifism is defined as the belief that any violence, including war, is unjustifiable under any circumstances, and that all disputes should be settled by peaceful means.
Modern day activist, would have us believe they embrace this belief. However, at the same time these very same individuals

will riot in the streets and hold up banners disrespecting the police, our government and our country.

This kind of activism is the highest form of self-entitlement and disrespects the world we all want to live in. It is a product of the Blame Game tactics which seek attention through misguided rules of engagement.

It is too easy to utilize statistics to prove how unacceptable any kind of activism today against the rules of law – can be substantiated as a valid and just way to confront any issue. The lopsided logic here is beyond insanity. It is in many ways nothing more than *Anarchy with Vanity*.

<u>Insanity is relative. It depends on who has who locked in what
<u>cage.</u>
Ray Bradbury

Chapter 9

Anarchy with Vanity

When groups of individuals gather to display disrespect for ALL police, based on the actions of a select small group of bad cops – they are taking liberties with regard to their right to demonstrate. Their anger, if it is indeed valid, is nothing more than an exercise with an ulterior motive.

The gathering to demonstrate against the law enforcement of our country, is in and of itself lunacy on a grand scale. The same men and women who take on the job of protecting us, feel just as hurt and insulted when one of their own steps over the line or out of bounds. To stand in the street denouncing law and order in a country that affords you the right to do so, is a conundrum.

Conundrum:
a confusing and difficult problem or question.

Not one law abiding individual does not sympathize with a victim's family when a member has been wrongly killed or incarcerated.
The problem, when ascertaining how someone is wrongly killed is a very difficult occurrence to diagnose today. The biggest issue surrounding such events stems from members of our society who will use these events to stir their own agendas of hatred.

Both sides being wrong can never result in making anyone or anything right. At the foundation of our national unrest on this topic is a very ominous use of racism being the reason for any killings. I am going out on a limb here – by viewing something entirely different than how the media reports any such events.

First and foremost, there's a double standard at play in any situation of violence, which serves to cause massive confusion with a difficult problem begging for questions.

Fear:
an unpleasant emotion caused by the belief that someone or something is dangerous, likely to cause pain, or a threat.

Two individuals placed in a situation filled with tension, both armed, will almost never result in one not getting shot dead or wounded.

The problem when sorted by some pundits of our media sources; automatically today place the blame on the law enforcement officials. Since this has become a means of reporting such events; members of our society feel it is their right to demand justice in a way that brings about chaos.

Bring in to the mix, government officials, more interested in getting voted back in to their positions and too often today are willing to dismiss any means of justice. Am I crazy to believe our law enforcement members <u>ARE *NOT*</u> members of a death squad hell bent on executing innocent men and women?

What kind of person would seek to become a member of law enforcement when they are viewed in society as being culprits? It is absolutely insane to embrace any idea which promotes such a notion. It is further embarrassing to imagine that civilians are all law abiding, peace loving members of our society.

There are extenuating factors which almost always are dismissed when occurrences of violence take place. In recent years, mass shootings have taken place on campuses, shopping malls, churches, temples and other places of worship.
By stepping away from the events, there's a pattern which can be inevitably brought to the surface as to why these acts of violence take place.

Our society has become inundated with idealisms that promote violent upheaval. When the government officials of our country cannot come to an agreement on so many different issues, related to poverty, mental health and education; it stands to reason these matters which yearn for a response will lead to violent acts. Of the key facts most relevant when associating how there is an upswing in mass shootings – a common denominator leads us to address the possibilities that the same people opposed to such acts; are also the ones enabling those individuals prone to such acts of violence.

Within the context of the problems that lead someone to hurt another person, the different issues listed above have effects we are not willing to accept.

How does a country, considered to be the richest and best with regard to supporting human rights have citizens living in squalor?

The official poverty rate is 12.3 percent, based on the U.S. Census Bureau's 2017 estimates. That year, an estimated 39.7 million Americans lived in poverty according to the official measure. According to supplemental poverty measure, the poverty rate was 13.9 percent. Annual standards for defining members of society who live in poverty is based on many different factors. For example, a family living in an area where the high cost of owning a house is $750K, gives way to statistics representing how many in the same area cannot afford to own such a house. The cost of living standards changes for many people based on different variables.

Poverty in the United States refers to people who lack sufficient income or material possessions for their needs. Although the United States is a relatively wealthy country by international standards, poverty has consistently been present throughout United States, along with efforts to alleviate it. (Wikipedia)

It is my feeling; statistics are skewed when depicting social issues. What constitutes someone to be labeled poverty stricken? There are men, women and children around the world, living in conditions that when read about or viewed on television depict the picture of **absolute** poverty.

We are shown the extended stomachs of small children, covered in flies and their mother's holding them with a look of extreme surrender on their faces. Our hearts go out to these people.

Is the picture we are being shown, while sitting in the comfort of our heated homes a moneymaker or a sincere request for help?

The world at large has deep seated roots that go back hundreds of years with such depictions of human rights being violated. In the 21st century, this issue should be the main focus of so many campus uprisings. Instead, the students of today are inclined to rally over whether or not an invited keynote speaker at an event has ties to a political party they are opposed to supporting.

The shame and sham of such acts further displays a madness our country will not easily rise above. It is my theory, the shame of these occurrences are products of our educational programs and policies. Many of the students who embrace the idea of protesting against one ideal or another are merely pawns in a bigger game. The students are of the mindset they want to be educated in the fields to which they feel their interest will make a difference. Many times, the educational process in place today is used in ways to confuse our younger generations.

The hierarchy in place at many of our learning institutions embraces the belief their past aggressions. of protest and anarchy are badges of honor.

The children seeking role models are easily swayed to follow such beliefs. They too want to wear a badge of honor that rises up against the oppressors of modern day civility.

At the outset of writing this book, there were and continue to be places in our world where real oppression is happening every day. Places like Hong Kong are in a constant state of upheaval. Students and citizens fighting for democracy against China communist rule are raging against the machine. What is at the foundation of these protests gets murky on our television screens.

These individuals are in a state of absolute unrest. These individuals are fighting to uphold a country's democratic policies while the multitude of citizens want to remain free under the guidance of their past expectations. A difficult concept to comprehend by American standards.
No one in America is at risk of having their freedom taken away. No one in America is in any way living in tyranny.
It is lunacy to believe otherwise.

The fears of the common American, is that we may not be able to afford the lifestyles to which we have become acquainted. The average teen wants to be respected and looked at with a semblance of acceptability. The madness associated with this need has been damaged in recent years. It is my viewpoint; our youth oriented culture is more inclined to label someone acceptable based entirely on what they wear – more so than what they believe or support.
The worst case scenario of this trend is easily displayed with regard to the upswing of gang culture across America.

Chapter 10

Gang Mentality

The delusions of gang culture have been a relevant issue for many years. The glorification of gangs has been an ongoing issue which has been a factor for generations of American families. The worst fears of a child becoming a gang member here in America has been a shared concern for parents since the beginnings of the 20th century.

According to Wikipedia, Gangs in the United States include several types of groups, including national street gangs, local street gangs, prison gangs, motorcycle clubs, and ethnic and organized crime gangs. Approximately 1.4 million people were part of gangs as of 2011, and more than 33,000 gangs were active in the United States.

Many American gangs began, and still exist, in urban areas. In many cases, national street gangs originated in major cities such as New York City, Los Angeles, Miami, Detroit and Chicago; they later migrated to other American cities.

It is still considered irrational for someone to become a member of a gang.

This does not stop Hollywood, Television, the Music Industry and other forms of counter culture to glorify the gang mentality. What is our youth being exposed to more often than not today? The theory can be posed that our countries sense of national pride and dignity are more likely to implode than explode.

When there is a constant embrace of anti-societal behaviors shown to be more acceptable than that of following the rules of law; our very foundations are being put at risk. It is being done in a ways and means most Americans can easily ignore. Under the guise of diversity, we are becoming more and more separated from one another.

The gang mentality often includes certain guidelines which when endorsed, makes a person who is accepted in to a gang privy to initiations and separate rules.

This practice has been in place for thousands of years. The manner in which any group can petition the allegiance of a person, plays on the oldest and most vulnerable aspect of the human condition. Our wanting to belong to something greater than ourselves has been a gang philosophy since the beginnings of war on earth.

There's a Safety in Numbers

There is an inability by any country to diminish the need of its people to feel safe. This statement comes with a caveat. The stipulations regarding what makes each member of any society feel safe are prone to different protocols and definitions. The very institutions that offer safety can be held accountable in ways that contradict the belief of what safety means.

When we hear about "gangs," we are immediately swayed to imagine a group of individuals' hell bent on creating chaos. This is a reaction groomed over time by recognition given to the negative acts performed by groups of men and women that do not conform to law and order.

I put forth the notion that any organized group can be defined as a gang. Any organization or institution governed by their own set of rules is in fact a gang. Under this definition, we can ascertain the different ways, our country is at odds with many of the same things which has guided and shaped us since our beginnings.

Under this definition, members who support a political party are members of a gang.

Under this definition, people of any faith are members of a gang.

Under this definition, individuals who support a sports team are a gang.

Under this definition, people who champion a cause of any kind are a gang.

The associations are endless, whereby proving the insanity as to why anyone would want to join a gang that endorses violence, when we are already members of different gangs in many ways.

The studies conducted as to why someone becomes a member of a radical gang have been ongoing for years. The illegitimacy of these studies only rely on the definition of "gangs" we have been lead to believe is the accurate assessment of gang mentality.

I understand this is a difficult concept to comprehend. I also understand it is difficult to embrace any notion that any of us are members of a rival gang.

And yet, on the grand stage of our national integrity, under the guise of supporting the rules of law, this is exactly the acceptance you and I are being told to embrace.

In the prior chapter I stipulated - *When the government officials of our country cannot come to an agreement on so many different issues, related to poverty, mental health and education; it stands to reason these matters which yearn for a response will lead to violent acts.*

I hinted at an explanation to better understand the definitions of poverty and how those living beneath the average income of most Americans can feel oppressed and in need of assistance. The members of this "gang" of underprivileged people have always been a part of the American society.

From the outset of our country's birth, there has been an ongoing growth in our population for those who took initiatives to better themselves. Often these people of wealth grew their enterprises in to mega corporations with far reaching effects on the communities they thrived in. Members of society who were not offered to take part in the growth, often fell by the wayside and hence the growth of poverty in our nation.

If we were to take a step back from this theory, as to how members of our population fell in to different categories; in a country that prides itself on the belief that all people are created equal - questions arise as to when things fell apart.

Did we fail to abide by the very rules we believed to be our designated truth?

Or did members of our society not have the wherewithal to follow the rules?

It is my belief; our country did follow their own designated truth. Our country did establish a ways and means to assist those less fortunate. Our country did abide by our forefathers want to establish a country with honorable and acceptable freedoms.

It is gang mentality to believe otherwise. It is insane to expect more water from a bottle quickly emptying. Which brings us to the issue of mental instabilities. The theory I put forth here incorporates the idea of our educational system being unstable as well. The obstacles in the way of moving forward as a country requires we better understand what is causing a rapid decline in mental health today.

More people today, the majority of them under the age of 30 years old, live vicariously through a personality they created for themselves Online. It is my belief; this personality they have deemed worthy of representing their every waking hour; further separates them from becoming the person they were meant to be. It is the same decay I have witnessed in men and women who have worked their entire lives, only to retire and stay inside their homes watching television all day. Slowly, they become so detached from reality, there is proof such inactivity related to social activities gives birth to diseases and loss of mental capacities.

They become so enamored of their freedom, it inevitably eats away at their hearts and mind. The tie-in with regard to this chapters take on *Gang Mentality* is a stretch. I agree with you.

However, the lack of no longer belonging to something these people can believe in has an adverse effect on how they can function in everyday society.

Whereby, our past generations, prior to the advent of the Internet, were not open to so many distractions; the elderly may have been prone to decay but the younger generations sort out his / her direction in life.

Today, because of the Internet – both our younger generation and our older generation are neck in neck with regard to losing their way.

The gangs may appear to have a safety in numbers, but they are both as weak as the other.

Chapter 11

The Great Divide

Since 2016, our country has been under siege. Never before in our history has there been so much divide. The ways and means behind this divide is sadly open to interpretation. There are those amongst us who feel justice is being served, and others who feel the principals and ideals which make Americans proud is under attack. Writers of articles and opinions, newscasters, athletes, entertainers, performers and late night TV hosts display their anger and applause for these events on a daily basis. At the foundation of what these articles represent is fear. The fears ironically are two-fold. One side feels that our country is being torn apart. The other side feels they are protecting democracy.

What serves to undermine or muddy the waters of 2020, is the desire for truth. Too often, Americans are fed opinions based on beliefs from the Right and Left. All we truly want and need, are opinions based on what is right and wrong. Sadly, our country is divided on what constitutes knowing the difference.

The very fabric of our nation's integrity is at risk. It is my opinion the recent Impeachment hearings can only be described as an attack by the Democratic Party on our nation's future. They have, in many ways become symbolic of the word: _desperate_.

It stands to reason that the vast majority of individuals who have allowed themselves to be swayed by rhetoric and propaganda fall in to a state of absolute desperation.

Meanwhile, the reality of our country's stability, with regard to employment, stock market activity reaching the highest numbers ever, and more importantly; the relationships between people of different races and religions are improving and getting better every day.
There are men and women in positions of power who will tell us otherwise. It is my feeling; these people will perpetuate hatred in vain attempts to separate a united country.

A party that once stood for the common decency for all people, looks and acts like the angry mobs of people who buy into their nonsense.

It is embarrassing to witness men and women, who represent our country in different capacities domestically and in foreign countries; put before a panel of elected officials who have spent the better part of three years chasing an elusive butterfly.

It is unfathomable, that hearsay and he said / she said conversations can be held up as evidence against any President, no less an average citizen.

The American people, those of us who still care about the *One Nation Under God* we all want to embrace; are shaking their heads in disbelief. Those individuals who are choosing to follow these modern day Democrats down a blind alley, do so at their own peril. What they are being led to believe is based on interpretation.

Our modern world, in many ways cannot abide by the rules of law passed down to us from our forefathers. We honor and appreciate their guidance through the years. Our Constitution has stood the test of time. It is now under attack by people who want to use the document as a testament to their own version of the truth.

A truth that is filled with a desperate need to appear as if they are in the right, when they are so sadly wrong.

At the birth of the 21st Century, the American people witnessed the levels of hatred from those not willing to embrace our ways of life. As the century unfolded, we have witnessed the unrest of our civil liberties, long ago established and buried along with the bigotry and prejudices our country feels forever scarred by.

We have witnessed a growing disrespect for our men and women in uniform who protect us on our streets across this great nation. These same men and women of law enforcement are as embarrassed when one of their own harms anyone undeservedly as we the people.

And yet, there are members of our government who want to keep the fires of hatred burning to enrich their own careers and pockets. I want to believe the American people can see through these acts of depravity and senseless violence. These same people, work side by side together with men and women of all races, creeds and cultural differences every day; without wanting to do harm to one another.

The siege is a desperate cry for keeping our country stagnated in the past, when in reality, we all want to move forward, toward a better tomorrow. We have never been given a better opportunity to stand united against such lunacy. In our modern times, the American people do not care about whimsical concepts related to the interpretations of our Constitution. In more ways than can be imagined, more of us want to know how a Vice President's son gets a job in a foreign country for a sum of money many of us will never make - based entirely on his father's status. We the people, who can distinguish such a wanting desire to know the truth behind real and actual corruption, are dumbfounded by people who seemingly wake up every day trying to find ways to undermine the status quo.

The morals the impeachment hearings attempted to sell to the American people was filled with sour milk. They are still trying to give us a bill of goods based on their own lost principals and sense of misplaced allegiance to their oath of office.

While they should be working for their constituents and helping to make a positive difference for our future; they are spinning tales of woe and pushing forth agendas that are no longer relevant to America.

They act like shocked school children who kicked a ball out of schoolyard only to see it get run over by a truck. They use puritanism as an act of justice, while hiding behind grimaces filled with hatred. What 2020 will reveal is something they could not have imagined. They have made themselves into a gang, who's members on the streets no longer want to follow.

Whether it be candidates touting fairy tales related to socialism or freebies for everyone; the intelligent American knows at the end of the day, nothing comes easy. No one deserves a free ride at the expense of taking something away from the people who struggle every day to take care of our own families.

What should happen, if the people in America who care about our future had a real say; is to give anyone who doesn't want to embrace the things we cherish, a shovel. Let them try to dig themselves out of holes before falsehoods and impulses bury them alive.

The American people know no one is above the law. The laws are no longer what we believe them to be. In Washington D.C., the laws change like the weather.

The disgrace of how our country has fallen prey to these scoundrels now reaches beyond the halls of justice. The everyday average celebrities feel it is their want to toss stones as well. They no longer perform or entertain. Instead, most carry on like clowns in a classroom; thrilled to call others names when the teacher is out of the room.

Our children deserve better role models. The past definitions of what it means to stand by a chosen political party are no longer applicable. The American people must adhere to their own sense of what is right and wrong.

Perhaps a new addendum to the Constitution is required. Maybe it could be put to a vote. It could read as follows: *It is right and just to pursue information that mandates someone / anyone in America is / was seeking monies to enrich themselves, family members or members of a group.*

It is further proper protocol for the President to withhold any monies or promises to a foreign country or corporation where corruption is suspected.

The rules of engagement have changed in every facet of our daily lives.

We cannot allow interpretation and hearsay to become a means of slander.

Chapter 12

December 18ᵗʰ 2019

"Hate, it has caused a lot of problems in the world,
but has not solved one yet."
Maya Angelou

"In time we hate that which we often fear."
William Shakespeare

"Hatred is the coward's revenge for being intimidated."
George Bernard Shaw

"I think that hate is a feeling that can only exist where there is
no understanding."
Tennessee Williams

"What is evil? Killing is evil, lying is evil, slandering is evil,
abuse is evil, gossip is evil, envy is evil, hatred is evil, to cling
to false doctrine is evil; all these things are evil. And what is
the root of evil? Desire is the root of evil, illusion is the root of
evil."
Buddha

"Hate is too great a burden to bear. It injures the hater more
than it injures the hated."
Coretta Scott King

"As long as you persecute people, you will actually throw up
terrorism."
Antonia Fraser

"Nothing comes of hatred."
Haruki Murakami

"...but no one was interested in the facts. They preferred the invention because this invention expressed and corroborated their hates and fears so perfectly."
James Baldwin

Say you got a real solution
Well, you know
We'd all love to see the plan
You ask me for a contribution
Well, you know
We're doing what we can
You want money for people with minds that hate
I have to tell you, brother, you have to wait
Revolution – The Beatles

The lunacy of American politics reached its epoch on this date. Since the day President Trump took office, the Democratic Party insisted they would impeach him. The ways and means of attempting what can only be described as a political coup reached the House of Representatives on this date. They acted like spoiled children.

Unable to face the reality of the 2016 Elections, the Democrats won their bid to impeach the President. The hatred displayed during the hearings leading up to and including the day long speeches made by those in favor of such an act, proved beyond any doubt, only hatred was a motive. During the reading of the final vote tally, the House Speaker, Nancy Pelosi can be seen snickering like a school girl who finally got what she wanted most in life – to oust the one boy in class who made her see herself in the mirror.

When asked poignantly about her hatred of Donald Trump, in what can only be one of America's greatest moments of ignorance and blunder – Nancy Pelosi harped on her being a catholic – she responded - *"I don't hate anybody," Pelosi snapped as she pointed and shook a finger at the reporter, James Rosen, a correspondent for Sinclair Broadcast Group who shouted the question as she was leaving her weekly press conference.*

She went on to say, "As a Catholic I resent your using the word hate in the sentence that addresses me. I don't hate anyone. I was raised in a way that is a heart full of love and always pray for the president," she said.

I am personally insulted by her standing behind a cloak of Catholicism to appear compassionate and understanding. The obvious disdain for Donald Trump, and all he represents has been a raging issue of concern since he took office. Such a statement should and must be viewed as an attempt to not appear desperate.

On Facebook, rants and raves took center stage. Members of my family posted their joy with regard to the impeachment. I did not wish to upset my own family members. I posted the above mentioned lyrics by The Beatles, from their song Revolution. It is in my mind an act of treason to interpret the Constitution of the United States to suit one's personal agenda. Furthermore, I think it is an act of war against the people who firmly believe what the President said or did is cause for impeachment.

I am convinced, through some kind of treacherous act, there are members of my family, and friends, who feel there is need for celebration were in some way, most likely during the course of their schooling or preferred company - were *Brainwashed.*

They will of course, consider this statement proof I am completely insane. That is their prerogative. I question their intelligence and knowledge of things of which they know very little. It is my firm belief, they embraced a vendetta against Donald Trump – based entirely on the same kind of misinterpretations afforded the Democratic Party during the aforementioned impeachment hearings.

I blame the liberal educators and the media. The liberal educators are in my mind, the degenerates' leftover from the 1960s and their protégés who have nurtured a revolution of their own based entirely on the hatred of America.

These individuals are large in number. They breed contempt while smiling at their own images in mirrors full of hatred and rage.

This is a day that will live in infamy. It has opened a can of worms so foul in odor, any future President will curse the day. The proof of the insanity, was displayed often during the impeachment proceedings. Many believe the spineless abuse of power by the Democrats will result in their own demise.

In retrospect, I have no feelings related to Donald Trump before he took office. He has always been in my estimation someone who was considered likeable or annoying.

An entire book could be written about what makes him likable or annoying. As President, he has challenged the definition most people have inherited over time regarding what a President should be like. The belief that anyone, including a President should be a certain way is amusing to me.

There are people who believe a President should be proper and dignified. They see the office as being inhabited by someone who exhibits their concept of what a President should act and be like. In our modern world, such a concept is out dated and requires a better understanding of human behavior. Is it any wonder the President of the United States when confronted on a daily basis by the media and those who dislike him acting in ways that many may consider unconventional? What makes any American think they can verbally abuse the highest ranking member of our Government?

Despite all the claims of America being a racist country, I personally never heard hatred towards Barak Obama when he was President for eight years.

If there was such a level of disdain for minorities in our culture, it stands to reason the level of hatred would have been exhibited during his administration. This statement is of course considered crazy by those individuals who have been _trained_ to hate Donald Trump.

If one were to ask the individuals who hate him – why they hate him, a variance of answers would most likely be shared. Some believe he stole the election in 2016. An analysis of how and why they feel this way can be traced to the interpretations of our electorate system.

I am of the mindset; the electorate system of American politics does what it has always done quite well. I am considered crazy to question, and I do, that the number of votes reportedly cast for Hillary Clinton in 2016 is a valid estimation of who actually voted for her. The idea of a conspiracy theory in this regard immediately places me in a category of being labeled insane.

What cannot be dismissed is the aforementioned concept by many people in America that because a woman was running for President, it was our duty to elect her. It stands to reason several issues can be raised related to who deserves such an honor.

I firmly believe there are women in America today, who are CEOs at large corporations or owners of their own businesses more capable of being President than Hillary Clinton. What Mrs. Clinton had was name recognition. What Mrs. Clinton had was an easy sell for the Democrats in 2016. There was an assumption, she was entitled to be President based entirely on her being a female and known for her tolerance and allegiance to Bill Clinton during his time in office.

Since 2016, there has been a movement beneath any campaign for any election in the United States. Feminism as a ways and means to ensure women are given every distinction they deserve in our society has been wrought with new levels of radicalism. What can only be called silly, has become a widespread industry of ridiculous expectations.

The most recent example of how far feminism has reached in to our minds with its toxic levels of expectation – we need only look at a recent production of A Christmas Carol, written by Charles Dickens in 1843.

The tale has been told hundreds of times. It has been fashioned to exhibit the Christmas spirit hidden inside all people.

It has been re-told with a modern twist many times. In the most recent rendition, released in 2019, the interpretation of the tale takes on a very dark and sinister example of what happens when agendas drive any story.

Without hailing or diminishing the production or that of the cast, several elements of modern society have been used to paint a picture of the main character, Ebenezer Scrooge – not as a miser without care nor concern for the holiday season, but instead as a much eviler person. This Scrooge not only is visited by three ghosts who in the story provide him with a semblance of redemption, his journey is displayed with acts of hatred for mankind beyond the story's original intent.

One scene in particular has Bob Cratchet's wife coming to him because she is in need of money to get an operation for her lame son, Tim. He sits and watches her degrading herself by stripping naked as an example of how far she is willing to go to get the money. He then advises her she is worthless. Upon exiting, she is given a soliloquy, whereby she puts a curse on him for all eternity. She ends her rant with a rather "fuck you" colloquialism that surpasses the acceptance of any kind of interpretation.

The film ends with her advising she will never forgive him. She then looks at the screen displaying a righteous look of satisfied vendetta against his soul.

Have we reached such a level of hatred in our society? I dare say we have when vindictive behavior is rewarded and women are exploited by the media as a means to attack men for every act of stupidity and indulgence. Indecency should always be on trial when one person degrades or harms another willingly. It is no longer about indecency or the ability to teach proper behavior towards others when only ignorance is shared as badges of honor.

Chapter 13

Globalism and the Double Standard

Globalism: the operation or planning of economic and foreign policy on a global basis.

Double Standard: a rule or principle which is unfairly applied in different ways to different people or groups.

The year 2020 will go down in history as undoubtedly being one of the most stressful years for many Americans in our history. More so than that of our forefathers, who experienced the Great Depression. This is I agree, a very contentious comment. I for one cannot actually explain how many of our forefather's survived such times. I would venture to say, many did survive through sheer determination to not allow themselves to fall victim to hunger, poverty and disease. Which makes the reality of America today, with our abilities to be in a position of affording in many cases all we need, and living at a time when our everyday sense of freedom is visible all around us; hard to compare to any time in history when struggle was the average American's experience.

However, the double standard expressed on a daily basis by those in denial of such comforts brings about a different reality.
When discussing this at any length with members of my own family – I have witnessed an inability to ascertain their own semblance of appreciation for the American Dream. Somehow along the way, they are quick to remind me, there is no such thing as an American Dream. Their standards are such, given their allegiance to agendas-first, that America is an evil empire.

They allude to things which in many ways are proof perfect of how easily any appreciation of American ideals has any value in their minds at all. The aforementioned "utopian" mindset has taken too many in our society by storm.

The word, "storm", is paramount when attempting to share a view that opposes the current "utopian" thought process. The storm I speak of comes from the adoption of many topics which are in theory good things to improve as both a nation and a member of the world's current societies.

Several years ago, I had a personal experience related to how globalism effects one's personal appreciation for America. While at a company with a business that enjoyed sales of their products all over the world, I was tasked with implementing a new computer system. The yearlong project provided me with a better understanding of every department's role in handling the company's objectives.
When it was time to change over to the new system, it was decided Veteran's Day would be the perfect day to celebrate the new formats and applications necessary to run the business.

I took it upon myself to decorate the office over the weekend while the system was tested and made ready for the staff. When they arrived on Monday, Veterans Day – the office was filled with American Flags, and a splash of red-white and blue banners everywhere. In my nearly 30 plus years as a computer networking administrator, there were no hitches or malfunctions of the new system. The phrase "business as usual" took on a new meaning with a system that provided enhancements and an overall better way of running the company.

I was called in to the owner's office at the end of the day. I foolishly expected to be applauded for the role my staff and I played in making sure everything went well. I was greeted with an entirely different lesson and viewpoint from the owner's perspective. I was reprimanded for decorating the office in red – white and blue. I was told, the company was an International company with no allegiances to the America in which I felt myself a part of. I was told to remove the "ridiculous" decorations.

Several months later, having felt the wrath of a "globalist" mindset, a young man entered my office who I had never seen before.
He appeared at my office door and looked around at my décor. He walked over to display on my wall where I proudly had my Honorable Discharge from the U.S. Army in a frame and asked, "What's this?"

Not feeling it needed any explanation, I commented it was my Honorable Discharge from my years in the military. He laughed out loud. He asked me, "Why would you want to waste your time doing such a thing?" I stood up from behind my desk and told him to leave my office. After making inquiries, I discovered he was a potential buyer of the company. I had spent a year readying the company for a new system and what I believed was a positive future.

The truth was far more disconcerting. The effort of installing a new system was just a ploy by the owner to make the company more appealing for a new buyer. When the new owners took control of the company, I was the first one to be dismissed. They were foreign investors with an eye to take the company toward a more global market.

The double standards surrounding any company's want to enrich themselves in the first decade of the 21st century was and remains a concern for the American dream. It stands to reason; many companies in America have made themselves richer by not wanting to pay the costs associated with running a business in America.

Why pay higher taxes and salaries when the same products can be made abroad for less? Why deal with the high cost of health care in America when little to no concern for workers can be exploited someplace else?

It is a difficult argument to make from a business perspective. Or is it such that the owners of corporations who endorse such decisions only want to fill their own pockets? Such decisions, in the grand scheme of the America we all deserve to embrace can be found in states where the removal of entire industries compromised the wellbeing and future of our citizens. The car industry, the same industry that bombards us with commercials every day; perhaps the number one advertiser in America today, abandoned the American Dream. Some of these companies are reportedly returning to America today. There is talk of new plants being built here in America. This will result in better opportunities for the people in those areas. Is all forgiven related to the many different ways their moving out changed the lives of people through the years?

Their double standard is easily defined with a simple – that was then and this is now – thought process. A standard based entirely on lining their own pockets with more money while many Americans faced difficult times due to such a mindless and selfish act of globalism mentality.

The results are far reaching and far more dangerous for all concerned Americans. When our rules of law are compromised, our national pride minimized and our not wanting to admit corruption is happening at the highest level of government by individuals entrenched in the system for too long; we are inviting the perfect storm for our future.

And those who were seen dancing were thought
To be insane by those who could not hear the music.
Friedrich Nietzsche

Chapter 14

Natural and Influential Hatred

While discussing any number of nuisances in the modern world, one that cannot be dismissed is that of violence. There are many different kinds of violence today. The worst of course, adheres to the deliberate harm of another person. It is very odd when we need to define any kind of violence as acceptable. Still, a case could be made that the abuse of power is a form of violence against the foundation of a country's core values.

A case has been made using the interpretation of the Constitution of the United States as the rule of law. While I can understand how the interpretations related to the conduct of the President might appear given the arguments made by Democrats during the Impeachment trial in the House of Representatives to be wrong. I have to take a moment to fully analyze his actions in our modern world as being acceptable while unorthodox.

Meanwhile, the actions and words issued from individuals who hate him on whatever grounds they deem plausible is highly suspect. Then again, could it be I am being exposed to the ways and means supporting the President - and individuals against the administration are only being influenced by their own resources of information?
I confess to being on the fence as to what makes all people adhere to their own versions of any truth. In the case of politics, it is akin to expecting a Protestant in Northern Ireland to fully embrace Catholicism.

It is akin to expecting sports fans to root for a team they have lived their entire lives despising. Many other examples can be shared explaining how deeply rooted the power of hatred in the world today.

The human race in my view, cannot rise above their hatred of others. While we are taught to be forgiving, expected to show the values of compassion and empathy every day; almost every time something disrupts that euphoria and brings us all crashing back to the daily reminders of human behavior. Sadly, every child is subjected to a form of what I will call – automatic hatred.
Natural hatred, I will argue stems from every individual's innate specialness. In a classroom full of children, not every child likes a peanut butter and jelly sandwich. This to me, is a natural hatred. More examples can be given with regard to how each person naturally likes or dislikes anything.

It is my belief, that when it comes to hating another person, much goes in to creating any ultimate disdain. Most times, it is the parents in every home; who will without wanting to encourage dislike of someone, end up influencing a child's natural hatred and gives birth to automatic hatred.

This argument can be made on any topic of interest in our changing world. Whether it the father's love of a sport or a team – inevitably it brushes off on the child. In some instances, a child can have no natural like of sports in general. A sense of foreboding may occur in these households. Then again, this example is way too broad to explain the actual appearance of something that is undeniably more about hatred of someone – than bothering to understand what is true.

In a recent article in the magazine section of the NY Times (January 5th, 2020) – an attempt is made to understand the ramifications of Brexit in Northern Ireland.

Brexit is the withdrawal of the United Kingdom (UK) from the European Union (EU). Following a June 2016 referendum, in which 51.9% voted to leave, the UK government formally announced the country's withdrawal in March 2017, starting a process that is currently due to conclude with the UK withdrawal as of 31 January 2020.

There have been conflicts in Ireland for thousands of years. To fully explain the levels of hatred between different sects of Irish people would require more volumes of books than would fit in any library. However, given there has been a somewhat agreed upon peace for several decades in the region; the discussions surrounding Brexit has brought back talk of the hatred thought to be a sad part of the country's history.

How hatred in a country can be maintained, while appearing to many to be in the past, is easily explained. There are individuals incapable of forgetting past transgressions. It is these individuals who ultimately strive to stir the pot in any debate about hatred.

Also, in America, it is well known that the educational system is labeled a liberal foundation. Whether or not, a family can instill understandings of respect for all people, places and things – inevitably our children are faced with an opposing viewpoint.

The opposing viewpoint can be based on actual facts or interpreted history. Our children are many times unable to ascertain any difference. Instead, they are graded on the facts and history declared the undeniable truth by the education system. Any opposition, by a student to challenge these facts or historical interpretations is met with disdain.

Education: *the process of receiving or giving systematic instruction, especially at a school or university. The theory and practice of teaching.*

A body of knowledge acquired while being educated.

An enlightening experience.

I find myself inclined to accept the second definition above to be more inclusive than the concept of learning derived from instruction or the acquisition of knowledge. In the first definition, the student is instantly expected to be taught what they must learn to become a self-reliant and well educated adult. The thought process of this being labeled education, in my mind, adheres to every individual on the planet earth in some way or another being indoctrinated to a thought process deemed worthy of everyone accepting the truth.

While, the thought of each person being enlightened to knowledge serves a much higher and more valuable means of learning what is true or false, and right or wrong. This chapter veers off the course of challenging what I believe is crazy.
I wanted to give an example as to how each person should be allowed to read what happened in any situation without being told how to view the content.

Whether it be history or science, the fundamental education of each child should be one that most importantly adheres to human behaviors. In every country, the mandate must be about what is right and wrong. Currently, as of the beginning of 2020 – a crisis is occurring in the Middle East. This time the crisis has to do with accountability.

The Iraq militia forces attacked the American Embassy in Baghdad. The threat to American lives was based entirely on a doctrine from the region of countries in the Middle East hell bent on destroying America. President Trump ordered a drone strike that killed one of the main terrorist in the region. Now the Iraq government has promised retaliation.

This back and forth is not much different than when children are playing. *It's my ball – No it's my ball – I'll take it and go home!* It's lunacy to see it any differently. No less, with lives of humans at risk – why does this keep happening to every generation?

One side will argue – President Trump is a war monger. He is by these same people labeled someone who teams with despots and murderers. The conclusion is made based on their want for peace. They do not recognize the threat to American lives. Their hatred is such that any reaction that results in violence can be avoided.

Should the President have waited until the Americans at the embassy were killed? In a game – and it is a game of power, individuals who threaten another person with bodily harm must be addressed in realistic terms.

I wish there was a way for someone to intercede in such actions.

I wish it was a ball being tossed back and forth and could be taken away sending each side back to their side of a schoolyard.

Bombs are not rubber balls. Bombs kill people. The truth dictates that the one who tosses the bomb first – in most cases survives the battle.

As insane as all this sounds, the key word in the explanation is the word – battle. We may have made a point in one battle, but the threat of war and harm to others persists. Many in our society would argue that another solution should have been discussed. How long do you wait?

There's an argument made in this particular example of abhorrence on a larger scale than the hatred of Donald Trump. The Middle East countries have embraced an educational process whereby America is taught to young children to be evil. Many children, from a young age are taught songs and chants to condemn America. Some students are conditioned to be martyrs for a cause. The cause ultimately deems they become terrorist. The terrorist goes so far as to ensure their family's will be taken care of by the government after they perform a suicide bombing.

Need we attempt to better understand what is bat shit crazy in our modern world?

Part II
DISCLAIMER

This book does not have the weight of a big publisher to ensure it will be read by anyone. A current book getting the push from publishers with reviews in the New York Times is titled "Why We're Polarized" by Ezra Klein. The embrace of this book is highly suspect and it represents a one sided viewpoint about what is wrong with America. Still, given the fact that Mr. Klein is only 35 years of age, his audience for the book is custom made for a book displaying the doom and gloom of American politics. His political viewpoints describe the United States in such a way as to imagine we are all going to hell in hand basket.

During the editing process of this book, my editors pointed out to me that the book is overly political. While I am amused to hear this criticism, I am opting to place this disclaimer in the middle of the book. I do agree that there are many different ways to display the crux of my theory related to how crazy the world has become.

I could harp on the obvious ways to prove my point, which for lack of a better explanation serves only to poke fun at things that in many ways – we may have become too used to.

> "Americans will put up with anything provided it doesn't block traffic."
> — **Dan Rather**

This quote can be found when typing in Quotes for Complacency on the Internet. It has become evident to me that our complacency has made many of us less perturbed by the insanity all around us.

Everyone can associate with the adage quoted above – whereby driving our cars has become in many respects more of an adventure in human behavior than reading about safari's or watching the latest episode of Alaskan truckers. Many people today are just plain rude. Common Courtesy has become a very rare trait when out and about in the general public.

Is it acceptable for large crowds of people to wait on line every year at Christmas – so they can take advantage of deals they cannot pass up? Every year we see videos or read about someone getting hurt because they were crushed by a stampede of people in dire need of a flat screen TV or the latest version of a phone.

Perhaps my editors are right and I should broaden my storyline about how insane society has become? To me, it's too easy to point out how dumb and ridiculous a lot of people act every day.

I would venture to say that much of what we may define as being stupid by others has been going on for a long time. But, oddly enough, while we have all been taught since childhood that we should learn from our mistakes, it appears nothing changes when it comes to helping members of our society rise above their need to be stupid.

The loss of common courtesy is a huge factor when attempting to pinpoint how deep the wounds of society today. If I were to try to figure it out – I would need to blame the Internet. It is of course very easy to blame a system or an inanimate object when trying to find fault with anything or anyone.

However, I truly believe there's a valid reason as to why the Internet contributes to our growing inability to be rationale human beings.

Within the context of the Internet – there's the underlying attributes associated with social media. We hear about social media today in many ways. The one glossed over part of how we communicate today has much to do with how we can voice our opinions and comments without any regard for who and what we are responding to at any given time.
The need for being polite goes out the window when we feel compelled to respond to anything.

The level of passion displayed by some people when responding on line is quite telling. Within moments of reading some comments, we are immediately made aware of their educational ineptitudes.
The need for profanity leaps out at us or we try to translate what is meant because a lot of people no longer know how to spell no less write a cohesive sentence.

What is even more amusing – albeit crazy, is how often any response can be dismissed because in some sort of unwritten law of online communication – Responses cannot be longer than three sentences. Anyone who chooses to write a lengthy response to anything is deemed a know it all or a trouble maker. It is quite stunning to be thought of as a know it all when many times the conversation is about something mundane and meaningless.

People today will argue about anything. If you posted a comment about how to make a peanut butter and jelly sandwich, it is very likely you would be met with several posts admonishing you. While I agree, peanut butter and jelly sandwiches are important – even worthy of hour long intellectual conversations, it's questionable as to how this could become a problem for someone.

One of the biggest taboos when communicating today, in conversation or when sending messages through our phones or computers is to avoid satire or sarcasm. These two very basic human ways of making light of any situation is no longer acceptable. Given this to be true, there are many writers and entertainers from our past who would have never been recognized or had their work published.

I have nothing but respect for you – and not much of that.
Grouch Marx

Those who believe in telekinetics, raise my hand.
Kurt Vonnegut

Sarcasm, the natural defense against stupidity.
Unknown

"At every party, there are two kinds of people – those who want to go home and those who don't.
The trouble is, they are usually married to each other."
Ann Landers

 Sarcasm is funny. It pokes fun at anything or anyone that can be described as taken things too seriously. Therein lies the problem related to our online comments and messaging today – we take ourselves too seriously. When attempting to drive home a point, inevitably it annoys people more than it can attempt to inform them or change their mind.

Trying to change someone's mind today is like trying to change a flat tire on a dark highway during a blizzard. We have all become stubborn and in many ways unwilling to openly discuss the weather no less the changing of the guard.

In the above mentioned book "Why We're Polarized" there's a definition given about today's writers – which I believe perfectly defines the many writers today for newspapers and magazines in America – *Explanatory Journalism. It is defined as being less about opinion and more about the exploration of ideas and policies.* The author of the article writing a review for this book in the NY Times was Norman Ornstein, who wrote "One Nation After Trump – A Guide for the Perplexed, the Disillusioned, the Desperate and the Not-Yet-Deported." In my view, it's unfathomable to have someone review a book which falls in line with his own take on the country we call home? When it comes to being fair and logical versus being condescending and partisan; it hurts to imagine what would happen if many of today's writers were writing policies for the nation's future.

identity politics: *a tendency for people of a particular religion, race, social background, etc., to form exclusive political alliances, moving away from traditional broad-based party politics.*

Much of today's criticisms about the American society is based on our being corralled in to predictable demographics and categories.

The thrust of such a definition makes it impossible for entire groups of people to rise above a definable and controllable set of standards.

This is the basis behind POLLS right before elections. An organization will call a certain number of people – 1000 to as many as 10,000 people. Given the response of this controlled group, the entire nation is supposedly represented. It's akin to old-school news reporters, who would years ago sit in a bar and by asking the patrons sitting around him about an event or person; would write articles about how entire neighborhoods felt towards everything.

It's madness to believe what POLLS tell us, because they are often tainted with questions to those polled to sway the opinion to what a certain group wants to sell the American people.

Are you polarized? I don't think of myself as being divided on many of the things we constantly read separates us. I like knowing my family is safe. I don't think the beliefs related to allowing people who have not been welcomed in to my country warrants an argument. I like knowing less people are unemployed. I don't think this deserves a discussion. I like that large corporations are being held responsible for abandoning America so they can make their products elsewhere. I find it offensive to buy anything that cost me more than it should when it's being made by people abroad who are being exploited.

When re-reading the above annoyance of being labeled polarized – I have to put on kid-gloves. There are many people who feel it is racist to not feel everyone is welcome in America. By using the word "welcomed" I am referring to the process in place that has always been a part of our border security. If a person wanting to become an American citizen enters our country legally, they have every right to pursue the American dream. Despite arguments opposing such a belief, I still believe in the American dream. The problem often dismissed by main stream America is a lot of people entering our country today have no understanding of what the American dream means to them and their families.

It is rather crazy to imagine the same people who hype about open borders would feel screening at Airports is no longer necessary? How safe would they feel sitting on a plane at 20,000 feet if everyone was awarded a free ticket and did not get checked at the boarding gate? Are these things political or logical in today's world?

Chapter 15

Homegrown

It has been reported that several colleges in America give special credit to any student who attends a protest. This kind of homegrown idiocy proliferates at the expense of exploiting our youth to act out against things many are not truly aware of or capable of fully understanding. The actual constitutional right to protest is questionable when those demonstrating do so for extra credit or because they are bored.

This book is not meant to be a political essay on what makes us appear insane. I will address areas where I believe we are as crazy in other areas of modern living. It is the homegrown aspect of how far reaching the madness is allowed to exist on a daily basis. Whether the influences are parental, educational or through technology to an unsuspecting and highly innocent minded child; we are ignorant to how far the depth of our shared perpetuation of hatred ends up hurting everyone.

I have shared the concept that hatred and thoughts related to disliking the President are influenced by liberal minded professors and teachers. This is not a new revelation.

I have spoken to or rather have been *spoken down to* by individuals who are perhaps of the aforementioned influential aspects of their upbringing.

Several of these men and women are in my humble opinion incapable of rationale thought. One person which I would be behooved not to mention is in my opinion one of the worst proliferators of hatred in American history. Jane Fonda, continues to find an audience for her disdain of America.

During the Vietnam War, she attained the infamous title of Hanoi Jane. She visited the enemy and mocked American Prisoners of War. She found an audience then and she has one today. She paraded herself out at the 2020 Oscars to announce the Best Picture. Who doesn't suspect the Academy, that gives out the once prestigious Oscar awards wasn't deliberately making a statement knowing the best picture was a first time award for a foreign film?

Ironically, we need not quote or look up images of celebrities or entertainers to understand the hatred of America. Many of the same thought process exist in every family.

I have been subjected to their hatred, which I must say – they consider entertaining. I have been in the company of some who deem it appropriate to put a picture of the President on a dart board beneath the words – Impeachment Party.
I have been in the company of relatives who burst in to outrageous proclamations wanting the President killed.

When asked what makes them hate him so much – there's a moment of absolute resolve. They first wait like wounded moths caught in a flame to see who will follow them in to the fire. Their disdain is so far rooted in believing their hatred is valid for obvious reasons, they truly cannot share their thoughts without finding themselves easily discredited.

I have heard stories from veterans whose children denounced them for taking a picture of themselves and their grandchildren in front of an American flag. This kind of homegrown hatred is not just upsetting – it is disturbing on many levels. Most often, the people who carry things to such lengths have no idea how hurtful and far reaching their misinformed hatred can be. They have been conditioned and riled up like a mob ready to hang anyone who doesn't agree with them.

It doesn't take much to get a crowd of people riled up today. Many people need to feel they belong to a movement that is sold to them as a crusade against tyranny. Are there different kinds of madness we don't know anything about? Actually there are more defined psychological disorders today than we can imagine. In a later chapter I define the growing number of disorders, which in the 1940s was a small pamphlet and today is over 1000 pages long. There's not much we can do about how many people are being influenced by insane theories and crazy ideas.

Ironically, at the root of promoting hatred, there appears a wanting desire for a lot of people to think themselves rebellious or characteristically seen as heroes.

Chapter 16

Sports

For the most part, I am guilty of trying to prove my hypothesis related to our being bat shit crazy while speaking of politics in America today. In many respects, there are far better ways of explaining how our society has gone off the rails. Perhaps, nowhere else are we drawn today in to a world of escapism from the daily madness then through sports. In the modern world, athletes are Gods viewed as heroes because they are good at something others are not as good at playing.

Baseball, Football, Basketball and the world's sport of soccer are the main examples of how "sports" influences our youth today. Other sports like Tennis, Golf and even Hockey enjoy world-wide appeal, but more so I believe it is these three – Baseball, Football and Basketball that are primarily the main sport entities that cater to our shared American interest.

When discussing baseball as a Pro sport, the 21st century has turned many athletes with an exceptional talent for playing ball in to millionaires. I do not begrudge any one of the many big names in the sport their due recognition for what they do on a ballfield. I do, however question the value of their talent when it is compared to the average citizen's self-worth.

Pitcher		Per Year	Avg. # of Games	Per Game / Inning	Per Pitch
Stephen Strasburg	7 years $245 million	$35 million	35	$1 million / 112K	$11k
Gerrit Cole	9 years $324 million	$36 million	35	$1 million / 114K	$12K

Batters					Per At Bat
Manny Machado	10 years $300 million	$30 million	150 games	$200K 22K	40K
Bryce Harper	13 years $330 million	$25.5 million	150 games	$170K 18K	35K

When analyzing what are currently the largest salaries in baseball today, it is to me highly suspect of how insane the owners, no less the players themselves might be to sign such contracts.

The above mentioned players, at the time of this writing are at an age when sports experts deem them to be at the peak of their talents. Given the validity of human capabilities with

regard to stamina, durability, and age related limitations, I find it quite fascinating for salaries to be given to any one on a sustained level of performance.
If the contracts determined the production capabilities on actual performance from one year to another – perhaps the high cost of gambling on any athlete would be understandable.

However, when a contract is given to a mere mortal based on what he's done in the past and is expected to do over a five to ten-year career, in my opinion is proof of insanity in baseball.

The largest case in point can be made with regard to how insane it is to me that any man or woman can make more money in less than one minute than it affords the average person to make in a year. Given my statistics above, Gerrit Cole, recently signed by the New York Yankees, starting in 2020 will make more money after throwing two (2) pitches in any inning than the average person on Social Security will make in one year.
Many will argue this is not a valid comparison. They will argue it is apple and oranges. I disagree because the cost of living in America is the same for every person.

| Basketball | | | | | |
Player	Salary	Per Season / Game 82 Games	Avg. PTs Per Game	Avg. Rebounds	Avg. No. of Assists Per Game
Stephen Curry	5 years $200 million	Avg. 60 Games $40 million /666K per game	Avg. 27 pts $24.7K per point	Avg. 5 per game 130K per game	Avg. 6 per game 111K per game
Russel Westbrook	5 years $206 million	Avg. 70 Games 41.2 million 580K per game	Avg. 26 pts $22.6K per point	Avg. 9 per game 66K per game	Avg. 8 Per game 73K per game

Basketball is to me, a fascinating sport to watch. I would not consider myself an avid fan; but admire the talent of those who can play it well. Here too, the highest paid players enjoy a salary that affords them to be very comfortable.

All athletes enjoy something above their salaries – which is ironically in many cases, provides them more money than their annual salaries.

As spokespersons for different athletic companies, they endorse products that make them in to household names for a product, above and beyond what they can do on a basketball court.

Football

Despite the relevance of other sports, Football is considered by many to be America's biggest sport. I would disagree, given my love of baseball as America's past time. I see football as being far less representative of how many can one day aspire to being a football player. Nevertheless, the popularity of the sport cannot be denied. During my time in the military, when based in South Carolina; on Friday nights, it was impossible not to recognize the popularity of football when an entire town shut down to attend a local high school game.

College football has been the mainstay of college fanfare since the 1800s, with mention of a sport **"ballown"** – an early version of the game, as early as 1820. In the 21st century, it is reported that Super Bowl Sunday is the most watched sporting event of any given year. In 2020 advertisers paid up to $5.25 million dollars for a 30 second commercial during the game.

I could stop here, when explaining my theory related to our being bat shit crazy, but will refrain from hoisting that flag.

When mentioning "a flag" – I allude to the practice
surrounding our standing for the National Anthem at every
sporting event throughout the country.

It was in my opinion, the disgrace of the NFL was exhibited
when a player, whom I will not even recognize by naming
him, wanted to draw attention to police killings of black
citizens. He chose to kneel during the National Anthem. First
and foremost, to appease those people who feel a kinship with
such an act as being anyone's right to do so here in America –
I call the act disrespectful and ineffective. I could list the
number of such "killings" and not wishing to diminish the
relevance of each lost life, call the protest nothing more than
self-serving.

I would of course be wrong to say so. The Nike corporation, a
company with a net worth of $160 billion dollars, made a
choice to embrace this same athlete as their spokesperson. In
doing so, they endorsed what can only be labeled an anti-
American credo as their company's definition.

I could harp on what any athlete makes when playing an
American sport, but I could never in good conscience
understand how any one athlete is given a world stage based
on their own sense of self-indulgence. On behalf of true heroes
in the civil rights movement, Rosa Parks and Martin Luther
King to name but two; I would hope many people see the
comparison of this one athlete to their sacrifices as appalling
to them as it is to me.

Chapter 17

The Entertainers

Christianity will go. It will vanish and shrink. I needn't argue about that; I'm right and I'll be proved right. We're more popular than Jesus now; I don't know which will go first – rock 'n' roll or Christianity. Jesus was all right but his disciples were thick and ordinary. It's them twisting it that ruins it for me. John Lennon (Interview March 1966, London's Evening Standard newspaper)

When and how it happened, entertainers today are by far the most influential voices in modern America. In 1966, the above quote from John Lennon was part of an article related to the Beatles, who at the time were the most successful rock band in the world. Their popularity lives on today, as part of a billion dollar a year enterprise within the music industry. When the interview conducted in England reached the shores of America, the backlash was big news for weeks in the summer of 1966. The all -encompassing rage related to John Lennon's comments caused many fans to burn their Beatles records and declare Lennon blasphemous. An argument could be posed related to how puritanical America wanted itself to appear in the 1960s compared to the all-inclusive mentality exhibited today. In a follow up interview related to the above comments, John Lennon said, *"I suppose if I had said television was more popular than Jesus, I would have got away with it."*

As a life time Beatles fan, the reaction by American media and religious zealots is quite interesting and further assists me in proving my point about our being insane. I will address the religious elitism angle in a future chapter, but for now will stay focused on the reactionary nature and power of media oriented influences when mixed with the lethal nature of the entertainment community.

Hundreds, if not thousands of similar examples can be shared with regard to how Hollywood and the Music industry have become a primary source of influencing world politics, environmental concerns, animal rights, and activism of any kind in direct contrast to actual beliefs and opinion.

Individuals *lucky* enough to reach a pinnacle position of being discovered or recognized for their talents are no longer looked upon as artists or performers; they are commodities. As commodities, they sell themselves as being representative of how their opinions should be respected and validated as absolute truth. The key word above is *"lucky."*

Talent is no longer an asset when seeking a life in film, theatre or the arts. Perhaps, many would argue – it never was. With the assistance of technology, albeit, Facebook – Twitter and Instagram, people who reach any semblance of stature as entertainers, immediately seek the underlying formula of advertising themselves like late night infomercial success stories found on the Home Shopping Network. The madness that surrounds the average person's need for devotion when subscribing to any performers lust for attention has become a toxic trait of our world view on everything, everywhere.

Narcissism

excessive interest in or admiration of oneself and one's physical appearance.

selfishness, involving a sense of entitlement, a lack of empathy, and a need for admiration, as characterizing a personality type.

self-centeredness arising from failure to distinguish the self from external objects, either in very young babies or as a feature of mental disorder.

In the 21st century, "narcissism" has seeped in to every home like a plague. The advent of social media has brought about the practice by millions of people to promote themselves with photos and things they find more important than concerns as human beings, we should embrace.

The selfish nature of believing their own opinions are more valid than any opposing opinion is met with hatred and condemnation. Issues related to empathy is almost nonexistent today.

Empathy

the ability to understand and share the feelings of another.

How lacking in common sense when discussing open mindedness today, many people act, is hysterical. It is comical to imagine a more exact way of defining entertainers today. To be clear, when talking about "entertainers,"

I am talking about individuals who have reached positions of being considered *face recognizable entities* in the entertainment community. As entities, their appearance in commercials and in magazine Ads sell the product based entirely on their being seen as popular or successful.
These very same men and women, only years prior to any breakout successful performances or promotion were struggling just like anyone else seeking a role in a film or a chance to perform on any stage.
The question, needed to be asked is:

"What turns the average person in to an over opinionated nut case?"

When listening to many of today's entertainers, inevitably there is mention of how much therapy they need to sustain their busy lifestyles. In other words, they are burnt out from exhaustion or most times a life of addiction to drugs or alcohol. I believe, their real persona doesn't buy in to the nonsense they support on a daily basis.

While many interests can be seen as necessary and may warrant applause; for the most part, the self-esteem of narcissistic people craves attention over integrity. It explains why any performer feels the need to speak out against anything related to something they believe will get their picture in the paper or part of the newest form of absolute power – a viral video.

If there is attention to be had, you can count on entertainers to comment or participate in some kind of public display. In America, we as Americans, embrace the belief that values matter. This is a statement that deserves explanation. There are different kinds of values today.

There are values that when shared with others represent concern and care for another's well -being. And there are a values that represent quality when buying a product or merchandising of any kind. The manner in which we buy-in to values of any sort, has changed since the birth of instant gratification.

People need to have their opinions validated. People need to consider themselves liked. The inability to achieve validation and acceptance by others leads to bouts of severe depression and feelings of public scrutiny. To the rescue comes an entertainer who adopts causes like people adopt cats and dogs. Their want for validation and acceptance is at a higher level than any average person seeking attention.

It is a vicious cycle that has gone in to hyper-drive since the arrival of social media. The manner in which our opinions and the interference of our daily sense of common sense has been changed, makes more and more people in our world today, lunatics.

I could easily make a list of the biggest culprits today in the entertainment world who aspire to their daily need for attention, but will reserve my opinion, so as to allow you the reader, to make up your own mind and list.

Once I talked to the inmates of an insane asylum in Hartford. I have talked to idiots a thousand times, but only once to the insane.
Mark Twain

Chapter 18

Global Warming

One of the biggest and most essential topics on the world stage today centers around the issue of Global Warming. The topic brings about discussions under different titles of interest:

- Climate Control
- Climate Change
- Climatization
- Environmentalism

A popular form of activism today has much to do with the effects of global warming. Thousands of articles and documentaries display the undeniable ways such a threat effects the future of mankind. Global Warming is a major concern on the world stage. So much so that Time Magazine named their person of the year in 2019, a 17-year-old from Sweden named Greta Thunberg who defines herself as an environmental activist on climate change. She has been nominated for the Nobel Peace Prize.

Climate Control is an area that in many people's minds lies between winning the lottery and fortune telling. Undeniably, there have been differences in the way our climate has effected weather related events around the world.

What gets lost in translation when discussing anything related to Global Warming, is the misconceptions related to our ability to reverse damages already occurred due to the possibility of man-made abuses.

The subject then is that of world pollution practices versus any suggestion we can control the weather or save the world. To many people, it is lunacy to suggest we can predict anything related to how the planet handles our *human* or the more popular phrase *carbon footprint*.

I am treading water here for what I believe to be obvious reasons. George Carlin was a well-respected comedian. During his lifetime, I would argue he went from being a comedian to being an observer of human behavior and world viewpoints. On the topic of Global Warming, he quipped:

"The planet has been through a lot worse than us. Been through earthquakes, volcanoes, plate tectonics, continental drift, solar flares, sun spots, magnetic storms, the magnetic reversal of the poles … hundreds of thousands of years of bombardment by comets and asteroids and meteors, worldwide floods, tidal waves, worldwide fires, erosion, cosmic rays, recurring ice ages … And we think some plastic bags and some aluminum cans are going to make a difference? The planet isn't going anywhere."

As the year 2020 began, in many places around America, new restrictions will be implemented for any business who dispenses plastic bags at the cash register for customers to carry what they purchased. The restriction cost to the average consumer will result in a five-cent cost for each plastic bag.

The plastic bag is not being removed as an acceptable receptacle for carrying the wares, it will now be an item with a price attached to it. The insanity surrounding such a display of environmental consciousness is beyond the comprehension of any one with half a brain in their head. The same efforts to combat "plastic" causing a threat to the future of the planet does not include a method for how when we go home – consume our groceries and place them in "PLASTIC!" bags to be carted away and dumped in to the planet. Is this crazy or some form of capitalism in its most profound form?

The stipulations related to Global Warming are not all comical and easily explainable. Scientist are actively attempting to discover why there has been an up-tick in temperatures around the globe.

Daily awareness on this topic is not the result of a 17-year-old environmentally conscious woman, currently being hailed by many to be the voice of global warming and climate control. To be fair, her activism and the relevance of her age does constitute a valid embrace by members of our society in need of a spokesperson; who on the surface does not appear to have an agenda or bone to pick with governmental agencies or corporations around the world. At fault for massive pollution around the world requires a unifying source which does not seek blame but warrants positive results. It is lunacy to imagine, even with regard to making improvements in how any nation addresses a need to take responsibility for their own pollution and how other actions of earth-decaying deeds end up as a form of bureaucratic corruption.

It is with this tendency that we can read George Carlin's skepticism with an open mind. On the surface, what makes a mockery of saving our planet, has its roots in the many different ways all nations seek short cuts when addressing problems that affect the national interests. Most short cuts are based on results that appear to be cost saving measures. Arguing both sides of this sensitive issue can end up sounding contrived without finding any solutions.

On the extreme other end of the Global Warming question, there are many who fear a far worse possibility. They question the validity of warnings like melting ice in the polar ice caps, record temperatures around the planet, weather patterns that result in massive flooding or uncontrollable fires around the globe with a much worse scenario.

These individuals feel the earth, as George Carlin remarks is a self-sustaining / self-correcting system that through-out time adjusts itself in accordance with its planetary existence in the universe. They feel the earth may not need saving in any way from us, but as a functioning part of the universe; it changes itself in accordance with a law of nature no human being can fully define or understand.

The average person who may or may not wish to embrace Global Warming as a valid topic of world responsibility needs to explain to naysayers why the weather services around the world often predict storms and rally support of devastating data modules that end up never occurring or being nothing compared to their forecast.

If we are to take the predictions about the world seriously, why is it questionable to believe whether it's going to rain on Opening Day of Baseball season or at a family picnic? If the weather bureau cannot get tomorrow or next week correct, how can we take what they say about the next 100 years to heart? It's a deafening need to make changes in so many ways, but most times it is madness for a select few to do what's right while others sit around laughing like they have all the time in the world.

Chapter 19

Homelessness

Homelessness is defined as living in housing that is below the minimum standard or lacks secure tenure. People can be categorized as homeless if they are: living on the streets (primary homelessness); moving between temporary shelters, including houses of friends, family and emergency accommodation (secondary homelessness); living in private boarding houses without a private bathroom and/or security of tenure (tertiary homelessness). (Wikipedia)

There's a 100,000-pound elephant in the room when the subject of Homelessness is discussed in America today. The immensity of the issue brings about scores of comments of empathy versus an equal amount of scrutiny by those people unwilling to agree with how the problem is being handled by government agencies in every state. The problems associated with Homelessness have been an ongoing problem of humanity for hundreds of years.

The growing movement toward social concern sparked the development of rescue missions, such as the U.S. first rescue mission, the New York City Rescue Mission, founded in 1872 by Jerry and Maria McAuley. In smaller towns, there were hobos, who temporarily lived near train tracks and hopped onto trains to various destinations. Especially following the American Civil War, a large number of homeless men formed part of a counterculture known as "hobohemia" all over the United States. This phenomenon re-surged in the 1930s during and after the Great Depression. (Wikipedia)

The historical ramifications of addressing the Homeless problem often displays a harsh and inhumane way of handling a nation-wide issue.

During the 1980s, the local church in my neighborhood set-up a shelter to assist with feeding and providing a place to sleep for ten homeless men each night. The organization of this service was developed by members of the community. Similar places and community centers throughout the five boroughs worked hand in hand with government agencies to organize these services.

The coordination of this service was handled with a sense of respecting how these homeless men needed to know they could be cared for in a humane and honorable way. During the years in operation, members of the community willingly volunteered to cook meals on a daily basis.

Local students were given school credits related to community service when they helped make beds up and serve meals each night. The services also included men and women who volunteered their time to stay with these men during the night hours from 6pm until 8am the next day. A bus brought the men from the city to the church each evening and picked them up in the morning. I volunteered to do the overnight shifts from midnight to 6am.

On many occasions, I had the privilege to discuss and meet with these men. During my time volunteering at the shelter, I noticed a similar pattern associated with why and how they became homeless. Every one of the men admitted to having had periods of drug abuse or bouts of severe depression. Every one of the men told tales of no longer being welcomed by their own families. It was indeed heart wrenching to hear these stories told time and again.

Despite their reliance on the shelter itself, these men were highly functional and self-efficient. They were served breakfast each morning before getting back on the bus to take them in to the city. They were each given boxed lunches which consisted of sandwiches, fruit and a beverage.

The city in coordination with the church's group in charge of running the shelter, subsidized the cost associated with buying groceries and necessary toiletries. The cooking, maintenance and daily up-keep of the shelter was handled on a volunteer basis by members of the community.

Without any semblance of regard for how well the shelter and others like it were being run by the communities in all five boroughs of New York City; the program was discontinued abruptly. Within months of the shelter being closed, talks began related to government run agencies taking over responsibility of handling the Homeless problems of New York City.

The subsequent response to the problem under the Mayor's office began in earnest with a different method of addressing the Homeless issues.

Homeless men, women and families were placed in Hotels at cost to taxpayers or into low income housing belonging to the City. Abandoned buildings are now being refurbished under a program to house the homeless in different neighborhoods throughout the five boroughs. The outcry related to this process has caused unrest and has brought substantial concerns by residents regarding the downgrade of property values in and around these shelters.

Anyone with an ounce of intelligence can see why this kind of Big Government involvement in such matters, serves to cloud the concern of these individuals by anyone who can make money off of their unfortunate situations. The exploitation of the Homeless, as pawns, should be a larger concern for anyone aware of how Real Estate is used anywhere in the country to address the growing issues surrounding the Homeless problem nationwide.

A much more perplexing argument can be made with how insane it is for governmental officials to "act" like they care while proposing methods and solutions that quite possibly garner ways of making themselves rich in the process. With regard to Real Estate, there are quite literally thousands of acres of abandoned buildings in Upstate New York. If the Government of any state actually cared about helping the homeless – these abandoned facilities could be turned in to <u>Centers</u> for assisting people to get back on their feet.

The suggestion of an all-encompassing solution is a radical idea. When housing the homeless for the sake of giving them a place to sleep, or as with the church run shelters, the homeless are in most instances put back on to the streets where they are inundated with reminders of their daily plight. A Center would provide a ways and means for many homeless people to benefit from programs created to help better themselves.

By definition, shelters are a place giving temporary protection. A center is defined as a place or group of buildings where a specified activity is concentrated. The solutions related to providing shelters for people in need of guidance and direction demands a different way of solving the problems of Homelessness nationwide.

It is unfathomable, that this kind of solution is not in place already. The Centers could house and feed the homeless population. The Centers could include classrooms with programs in place to help these people get re-acquainted with being respectable members of our society. If rehabilitation centers are in place to assist members of our family in need of recovering from drug addiction and other personal problems, why is it not a remedy for helping the homeless?

Under the same program, jobs could be given to those members of society with skills to assist each Center's purpose. The solutions would benefit each state, solve the homeless problems in a better way than to have members of our society shuffled around like cattle on a ranch.

Such a program would require government officials in each state to put aside their petty indifferences. Such a program could receive funding based entirely on the overall validity of addressing the problem of Homelessness. Programs could be put in place to solve the issues, instead of placing a temporary Band-Aid over a worsening wound.

This kind of proposal would require organization and diplomacy. Ironically, two ingredients not found in state run governments today. Sadly, two acts of humane behavior those in charge most times cannot come to terms with at any level of common sense. It has been the practice of our government officials to throw good money after bad whenever there is an opportunity for funding to be misused and handled in ways that cannot be traceable. In other words, corruption in many ways is the main issue when addressing social problems of any kind in America today.

Our elected officials may start out being crusaders for any cause to help society. They are soon tarnished by the different methods in place for many years that provide money for individuals who may as well be members of organized crime.

The decisions now in place to legalize marijuana in America proves my point. Marijuana, pot, weed or any name you prefer to call this drug has been illegal in America for generations. People have been incarcerated, with some serving life sentences for distributing marijuana. Here in the 21st century, the government is taking the position that marijuana is a recreational drug. The changeover from one mindset to the other can be traced to several factors.

First and foremost, the government's take is related to what I will call a new attitude. The new *"If you can't beat them, join them"* mentality stems from a more broadmindedness pronouncement of how to address an issue; that quite frankly confesses an inability to control substance abuse by our ever growing population. The more obvious change of mind with regard to legalization has to do with the ability to make money. Why chase after street distributors of a substance when the country can benefit by selling it legally? Taxing those who wish to sell marijuana will give way to a growing industry here in America.

The mindset in an even maddening sense provides a ways and means to eliminate the middle man. It is in some ways; the first program change which will eventually become the sale of all drugs to the public without any real concern to side effects on any member of society.

The proposal of Centers brings about a different way of addressing the problem of homelessness. Many in our society may view the Centers as Institutions, which over the passage of time have become associated with reputations of putting people away. This is not the case when individuals require assistance related to drug addiction or the many other aspects of requiring help in regaining their place in society. The idea of helping those in need demands we seek to solve the problem on a grand scale.

There's a growing concern that the Homeless men, women and children of today are pawns in a much larger scheme to find different ways to make money for and give speaking points to government officials unable to solve problems. Is it insane to suggest, any social issue in America and around the world can inevitably become a money making enterprise? Is it madness to believe the Homeless problem is really the after effects of failed government programs? After closing facilities and discontinuing programs in place for many years, the government agencies were declared obsolete. Institutions where challenged people were housed and cared for became too expensive to keep open. In reality, the size of the facilities could no longer handle the growing population of those in need of their services.

The government chose to close these institutions and put out to pasture the many who are in need of the services rendered. Why is there no outcry for recognizing this travesty of humanity? In America, if there's money to made in any way, we can be certain, our officials will sooner or later profit from the problems of society.

Chapter 20
Speculative Journalism

Speculative:
engaged in, expressing, or based on conjecture rather than knowledge.

Journalism:
the activity or profession of writing for newspapers, magazines, or news websites or preparing news to be broadcast.

fake news:
false information that is broadcast or published as news for fraudulent or politically motivated purposes.

HuffPost (formerly <u>The Huffington Post</u> and sometimes abbreviated HuffPo) is an American news and opinion website and blog, with localized and international editions. It is edited from a left wing political perspective.

According to the website – the term "fake news" was originally labeled "false news." The origins of such news dates back to the late 19th century.

Early on, when newspapers were the go to source for information; it became common practice to get a reader's attention by promoting the purchase of a paper with sensationalized headlines. The better a headline, the more likely a reader was to purchase the paper.

The basis of truth surrounding any article slowly deteriorated with regard to integrity displayed by the paper or the reporter writing the story. If a story amassed a higher readership on a daily basis, sensationalism trumped the legitimacy of journalism every time.

"You know I used to admire reporters, they wore clean shirts, clean ties, doing something – and I wanted to do something, but you know what it's like, it's like they ask you to go out every day and see people at their worst, that's what it's like."
Michael Parks as James Bronson
In the short-lived TV show Then Came Bronson

In 1969, the TV show *Then Came Bronson* depicted a character who at the beginning of the Pilot Movie for the series is shown in a newspaper office. He is berated by the paper's Editor for writing a story about a fellow reporter (Martin Sheen) who committed suicide. The weekly series from 1969 lasted one season. Each week, Jim Bronson played by Michael Parks represented a free spirited romp on motorcycle across America. It was a show, that despite its negative commentary about journalism made me want to become a newspaper reporter. It also made me long for the wide open spaces of the American heartland. I pursued the "journalist" dream, but learned early on just how correct the quote above was about journalism.

Very few news reporters since 1969, or writers for that matter of any journalistic live to write beyond each publications agenda. The agendas subscribed to by the owners of written material in America, do not subscribe to the one adage that affords them their right to be in business.

The one adage being from the Constitution of the United States – which states: *Congress shall make no law respecting an establishment of religion, or prohibiting the free exercise thereof; or abridging the freedom of speech, **or of the press;** or the right of the people peaceably to assemble, and to petition the Government for a redress of grievances.*

The origins of Free Press according to the History Channel website declare - *Before the thirteen colonies declared independence from Great Britain, the British government attempted to censor the American media by prohibiting newspapers from publishing unfavorable information and opinions.*

One of the first court cases involving freedom of the press in America took place in 1734. British governor William Cosby brought a libel case against the publisher of The New York Weekly Journal, John Peter Zenger, for publishing commentary critical of Cosby's government. Zenger was acquitted.

As newspapers become less and less relevant, due to the many more people getting their daily doses of news on-line; the newspaper industry in recent years have taken to endorsing agendas over the integrity of any truth and fact based storylines.

Mainstream media has followed the same shift when reporting most stories. I call this shift, *Speculative Journalism*. The trend reached its epoch during the 2016 campaign for President. It reached its current state of speculation over actuality or reality after the election.

When Donald Trump won the election, he created a tailspin in news reporting around the world.

The legitimacy of National Polls which up to election day 2016 had Hillary Clinton winning the election, caused what can only be described as widespread panic throughout the journalism world.

The result has been something of a revolution for journalist. They either harp on being right or angry idiots proven wrong. The sad part of this revolution is not about truth, justice or what was once hailed as the American way of life; instead, it has been the loss of intellect related to our integrity.

Never before, in the history of the written word, has America been more divided by what they choose to read or watch on TV. The two divides have created a chasm so deeply removed from believing what is right or wrong; our daily lives and opinions are subject to being scripted reality TV shows – of which most American's embrace as truth based entertainment.

Any story that can be based more so on a writer's opinion than that of fact based information is "Speculative Journalism." When one paper can present opinions to its readers, who sadly have fallen prey to accepting any information as factual, rather than seeking a balanced objective, the paper is practicing Speculative Journalism.

The seed of this kind of news reporting falls in to a much deeper well.

Why is the media so liberal and biased?
Causes of Media Bias Media bias can happen due to **various reasons**. It occurs when journalists (or people) connected with the reporting of a particular event, have a **prejudiced opinion about certain things**, which ultimately results in a distorted version of the story.

The key word in the explanation above is "distorted." It is a very whimsical word in today's society. Simply translated, the basis for stories are subject to interpretation over that of any facts or reality based observations. How this translates to our ever getting at the truth becomes victimized by our individual desire to believe what we choose to believe is right or true.

Quite ironically, a further in-depth analysis of speculative journalism can be compared to our religious beliefs. The media in this concept – has become for many, our news related God. As crazy as it may sound, more people subscribe to their versions of the truth, foretold to them by the source of news they deem trustworthy every day.

The purchase of a newspaper, magazine or subscribing to on line blogs – down to what news channel we watch, dictates our want for the truth we want to believe in. The divide is akin to how we want to embrace or denigrate the existence of God.

Of course, I completely understand the comparison sounds insane.

However, the truth of the matter, in my way of comprehending how many different versions of the truth can be understood by two people, a group of people or large segments of our society cannot be explained to me any better.

The same end result becomes obvious to me – when discussing what I believe to be true versus another's opposing opinions. It used to be when in the company of a mixed group of people at any gathering, we had to avoid talking about sex, religion and politics. Today, the taboo subject to avoid is always politics. While, in the past, the topic of politics could lead to polite dismissals like "let's agree to disagree." Today, all-out war erupts around family dining rooms. No longer can any individual express his / her opinion without expecting to be berated.

Do we all need to do what the Michael Parks character did in the series Then Came Bronson? Get on a motorcycles and disappear in to the American heartland? Speculative Journalism has turned many Americans against one another. It is a disease that cannot reverse itself with expectations of any cure.

In a much hailed book "Why We're Polarized" by Ezra Klein – he is credited with labeling today's writing as "Explanatory Journalism" which is defines as being non-opinionated and based on facts. I would challenge this viewpoint with regard to my defining these same writers as practicing "Speculative Journalism."

At the heart of this difficult reality, we have to rely on the journalist students of the future to unravel the mess. Sadly, they are mostly being educated in institutions where a single mindset rules the day. It is more challenging to maintain one's personal integrity in any institution that subscribes to its own version of truth.

When researching "Why are most colleges in America liberal" – the open ended responses do not represent an actual and reliable definition. Immediately, when reading the responses one can easily ascertain there is an animosity by conservative minded individuals against the institution itself. The most quotable response is that of professors all being liberal. Which in and of itself is in my opinion, an overzealous and dismissive generalization. However, to be fair, we do live in a society that chooses to cancel any opinion or thought process not in keeping with popular opinion. In the next chapter, I will discuss an even more ridiculous trend practiced in America today. The fear of being "cancelled."

Chapter 21

Cancelled

To be **Cancelled** in America today, means to dismiss something/**somebody**. To **reject** an individual or an **idea**.

What is quite telling related to our national divide can be found in the origins of self-esteem. While there are nationwide objectives in place to curtail bullying in our schools and workplace; hardly anything can be achieved if we do not first and foremost instill in people the importance of understanding the difference of opinions we all subscribe to.

The dismissive nature of many people who cancel one another over anything they do not wish to better understand is remarkable. What is more fascinating; being how silent many can become when challenged by an opposing opinion or action. In every industry today, whether it be our workplace, our chosen favorite sports team, celebrity or any other related form of interactive event or belief system – most people choose to remain neutral when surrounded by others.

The Cancel Culture, like the practice of Speculative Journalism supports only one way of thinking and acting as being acceptable. It is in many respects a higher form of bullying similar to kowtowing to the biggest kid in the schoolyard. Any teacher, in any school will undoubtedly share stories of maintaining order when there is an obvious student population wanting things to be a certain way. The ways in which each teacher views the population in question becomes an interesting study in maintaining order and an acceptable balance.

When a teacher chooses to take a side in any way, on any issue, she / he declares themselves part of the Cancel Culture. If a balance cannot be found, chaos ensues. Every teacher is first and foremost human. They all, without exception, have what I would call one of the most difficult tasks anyone can choose to accept. When one teacher chooses to circumvent any necessary balance, they risk causing a divide in the classroom and become advocates of the same kind of bullying they try to prevent every day.

The biggest display of "cancelling" today is visible in the entertainment business. Whether or not we as an audience want to admit it is possible – celebrities represent a portion of society who are not judged or held to the same standards as others. There is a hierarchy in Hollywood, Nashville, and the music and sports industry at large. The people who entertain us in many respects also disdain us. They each have their own brand and consider themselves to be a commodity for sale. When they reach a certain level of recognition or status, they become more dismissive.

Ironically, we as an audience seek to be entertained at any cost. In some ways, our allegiance to an actor, actress, singer, band, player or team erases our ability to understand all of these people are just human. It doesn't stop us from clawing at one another to get a picture of ourselves standing next to these people. While they can easily dismiss us, many become more obsessed with being near them and knowing all we are led to believe makes them in to super beings.

In America, billions of dollars are spent each year on idolizing our entertainment industry. Corporations have budgets that cater entirely to sponsoring these people. In a heartbeat, what was popular yesterday can be canceled tomorrow simply by who wears what or how they act in the public's eye.

Sponsorship is BIG Business. Nowhere is it more evident today than the Sneaker industry, fashion industry and car manufacturing. Athletes wear their own line of sportswear. Sneakers make up the largest form of endorsement contracts today. Air Jordan sneakers can fetch thousands of dollars on eBay. The desire to own some sneakers has resulted in death when released at outlets throughout America. Articles abound in newspapers related to people, mostly children being murdered over a pair of sneakers. Sports Illustrated depicted a front page story "Your Sneakers or Your Life." *In May of 1989, 17-year-old James David Martin led 15-year-old Michael Eugene Thomas into the woods, strangled him to death, and took his two-week-old pair of Air Jordans.*

Chapter 22

Health Care

One of the most talked about topics in America today is Health Care. The Health Care industry is a highly diverse umbrella. The industry, can be defined by hospitals, clinics, offices run by conglomerates to your local or primary doctor's office. Within these health related facilities, the men and women who are dedicated to helping us stay healthy deal with an obstacle. A course of rules and regulations that govern how they work.

The madness of the labyrinth they have to walk through every day when trying to keep us healthy is at times impossible to navigate. Most studies or politicalized issues surrounding health care are reported from a health industry standard. Who controls how we are looked after medically is more important than how good or reliable the care itself.

Throughout this book, I have attempted to share examples where I feel we are all being forced in to some kind of an asylum. The madness that surrounds health care is in many respects toxic. It's a damned if you need it to a damned if you don't kind of paradox.

The issues surrounding whether or not anyone has healthcare is not a universal problem. There are countries with socialized medicine. This translates to citizens in those countries getting free health care. Is it free? The word "free" gets bandied about as a sure fire way to attract our attention.

In the countries where socialized medicine is popular, there are creative methods in place to subsidize the medical profession with taxes or budgetary constraints. The constraints can be quite liberating for some and like here in America, very expensive for others. This highly complicated issue has over the course of many years become a political debate issue.

The insanity related to politicians discussing health care is like asking a tree to decide what birds are allowed on its branches. Here in America, individuals have to pay huge amounts of money for their healthcare.

The buy-in to this method of securing a health care plan that suits you or your family's needs can be taken care of properly should anything go wrong, is like gambling. When gambling, the average person attends a casino with the notion it's their lucky day. The cliché related to gambling in such a facility has and always will be - the house always wins.

Thus, is the case when paying for health care in America today. Upwards of $1000.00 a month or more can be doled out for health care by some families or individuals. The chance of anyone needing to spend $12,000.00 for their health care needs in a given year is very remote. Hopefully, they will stay healthy and require regular doctor visits to ensure they are doing fine.

This kind of national abuse on the American household is greatly debated as to why such a cost is considered valid versus any notion it is larceny. I won't go into the specifics surrounding this madness.

I will ask that you the reader fully understand the rationale behind it needing to be mentioned in this book. The background battles behind health care is widely discussed, although in many respects a large portion of our society takes the need for it, for granted.

Those individuals who are gainfully employed, enjoy a perk of having a job that pays for their health care needs. The cost of annual health care is often mentioned when they accept jobs today. Human Resource departments today go so far as to advise new employees their salaries include the cost of health care. What becomes quite ironic and typical of American industry today, is the receipt of our pay vouchers for work and noticing deductions that include cost of maintaining your health insurance. This roundabout way of informing members of a company they are part of company health plan while charging them to maintain it through weekly or monthly deductions from their salaries is blatant high way robbery.

Worse off, are men and women who lose their jobs before any ability to get assistance from the government (I.e. Unemployment Insurance or Medicare). These individuals must adapt their budgets to ensure they can afford health insurance. The vicious cycle is maddening and can lead to people needing health care they may not have ever needed had things been better planned for or made available to them.

Health care is like an umbrella. Do we need it during a little shower? Do we need it when all hell breaks out? The choice is not open to discussion in a society that maintains you have to pay for it whether you use it or not. Like car insurance, those of us who drive safely every day live longer but it cost us a fortune to stay on the road.

The other primary factor related to things being out of whack in the 21st century has all to do with how invasive the overall Health Care industry is with regard to access in to it everyday life. Television and radio commercials are filled with Health Care related advertisements.

Whether it is drug Ads or the ridiculous nature of modern times, one hospital claiming to be better than another; these Ads run night and day 24/7 on every public radio station and television. From Erectile Dysfunction drugs to multiple commercials related to the handling of Diabetes, Alzheimer's and main stream disease control.

The hypocrisy of making drugs comparable like the buying a car is horrendous. All Ads come with disclaimers and advice to ask your Doctor if the product is good for you. The most disturbing aspect of these commercials is the sped up dialogue at the end of the commercials on the radio or the impossible to read fine print on the TV screen – whereby along with a voice-over the narrative provides warnings about the side effects of the drug on "some" users – which includes the worse warning – could lead to death. This is madness on a level that cannot be fully defined.

Hospital: *an institution providing medical and surgical treatment*

and nursing care for sick or injured people.

Not so in the 21st century. More and more hospitals are now declaring themselves Specialist in a given field. Doctors are now affiliated with hospitals that prescribe to their particular specialties. The competitive nature of health care is alarming on many levels.

What constitutes any level of trust for our health and well-being when hospitals like corporations base their bottom line on solicitation?

Solicitation:

> the act of asking for or trying to obtain something from someone.
> the act of accosting someone and offering one's or someone else's services as a prostitute.

Which definition best defines modern day health care? Are hospitals today in the business of seeking sick people as if they were customers? Several years ago, hospitals under the guidance of non-medical CEOs and corporate heads were instructed to view all patients as clients.

The standard of how each person is treated has been under scrutiny for decades. Each ailment, injury and disease has a standardized limit in every hospital. The Health Care industry has put in place a ways and means to pay for each person's care based on their own calculations for how long each person should be cared for. The client – customer – albeit each patient is cared for like a used car. When a new car leaves the lot, the thought process is, it loses value. When a patient enters a hospital, the hospital is paid up to a number of days for each person's specific health related issue. If a person needs longer terms of care, the hospital loses money.

This kind of madness can and will only get worse. When hospitals are given selective power related to who and what they can treat, to boost the credibility of their stock holders and investors; they risk the basic premise of their original purpose.

When commercials on our radios, televisions and databases become nothing more than comparative narratives related to our health – we have a humane problem far worse than refused medical treatment. We have chaos that borders on actual and real oppression. This may sound crazy, however, I will argue; how can it be that people of a higher class in our society – albeit the rich and famous get the best doctors or best care based entirely on who they are? The same care should be available to every citizen on an equal basis. No hospital should have a tag line that boasts of the best healing record or highest number of success cases for treating any disease.

Such claims, in my mind, prove my point. If health care cost so much for each person and their families; the same level of services and care should be available at every facility, we need to utilize.

When board members at hospitals make salaries that are five and six times the salary of the actual men and women, nurses, who do the actual caretaking of our sick; there's a form of exploitation that nullifies any claim the hospital has our best interest in mind.

When doctors, surgeons and specialist alike – denigrate nurses as if they were nothing more than hired help in a horse clinic, there's a form of abuse that warrants investigation.

Chapter 23

Accountability

What if there was a way for citizens to make decisions on how tax dollars are spent? What if, by using technology, a select group of citizens could vote on how the government spends money? Every facet of our tax dollars are spent in ways which, we as American citizens have no way of controlling. Politicians can take funds from a budget and spend it in any way they deem necessary.

It is not so farfetched to imagine a future whereby citizens require accountability in more ways than available to us today. It is insanity to fully rely on men and women who deem themselves worthy of our trust while in many ways making back room deals to further their own careers. A cry for term limits based on how long anyone can serve in congress needs to happen, or like history itself, the same forms of corruption will be repeated again and again.

When we hear of politicians who have been in office for decades, they can no longer represent a clear and concise concern for their constituents. Instead, they become as steadfast as any person trying to sustain a career in a field they were once very good at a long time ago. This accusation, is controversial on many levels. First and foremost, I make this claim based on the decisions being made today throughout the government, and by public and private company's everywhere.

A double standard is in place that is diabolical in nature. A government official, who has been in a position of power for as long as they want to be, questions the validity of our elections. Surely, there has to be checks and balances in place to make these officials accountable.

When company's make decisions based on the whims of CEOs who make sums of money each year that calls in to the question the validity of the company's net worth; a problem has occurred that brings to mind the kind of structure known during medieval times. The CEO in effect becomes the ruler of his or her domain. The workers in this scenario are no longer viewed as members of any company; but are treated like surfs responsible for catering to the whims of a ruling class.

This kind of madness has been in place for more years than anyone can truly and fairly define. When looking at accountability as something which is a valid way of maintaining integrity, we begin to realize how the lack of accountability can easily lead anyone astray. I imagine, over the course of our lives, we have witnessed many times, a form of restructuring used by politicians and company executives as a means to make us excited about new ways to do the same thing.

This very manipulative form of motivation is akin to Kings of ancient times promising more bread or higher wages to his kingdom. The comedy of these promises is the same kind of deception we have embraced throughout the world.

Such promises made by leaders, or heads of billion dollar corporations are made in a way that sounds great or reads well in a memo – however, the gist of the promise is based entirely on more of something and higher wages for someone who actually makes the bread itself. In actuality, we as workers, as citizens applaud our own capabilities which we lose sight of doing when used by politicians and CEOs like pawns on a chess board.

This may sound vindictive to some, or raise an eyebrow by those of you who follow the train of thought based entirely on common sense. It was not until the beginning of the 19th century, during the rise of the Industrial Revolution that our education system became organized, structured and standardized. The mandate in place is easily researchable. In every country, an educational standard was adopted to best educate the populace.

The accountability related to the education system gave way to the highest forms of education available to those people who could afford to be educated. This is important to understand when adhering to accountability versus availability. Here in the United States, it became necessary to send children to school. Every child, when they reached a certain age was required to be educated. The format for their education was set in stone. Each student was / is to this day required to learn how to read, add, subtract and multiply, learn history and science -- and if they are good little boys and girls, as a treat, they will get classes in art and music.

As the education systems flourished, different forms of availability were put in place. Religious institutions sprung up in every country, whereby religion of every denomination began teaching different beliefs and interpretations of the Bible. As these institutions grew, a different standard was introduced in to the communities around the world. The standard was introduced to the people as a form of better educating each child. Hence, the introduction of tuition was created to illustrate to the people – if they wanted a better education than was available in public institutions, they had to pay for it. The format for making this more appealing was the presentation of uniformed teachers (nuns, monks, brothers and priest) – who as representatives of the Catholic Church looked like the best suited Army for helping any child reach his / her potential.

Further appeal was made more relevant when each child was required to wear a school uniform. Once indoctrinated in to the formula for success, deemed a higher level of education, entire communities throughout the world considered the accountability of such institutions to be the best means for educating their children.

An argument could be made that private schools do in some ways educate children in ways that are not required in public school facilities. Ironically, the only real difference is the exposure to religious or elitist idealisms. Also, in place is that of discipline – whereby many believe a student is without question held to a higher level of accountability for their actions and ideas.

I am a product of a catholic school education. When I think about this from an abstract perspective; I am first and foremost appreciative that my parents spent their hard earned money to send me to school. I am aware that what I learned and how I learned was formulated by a strict and highly structured means of educating me. However, I am also aware – many of my childhood friends did not attend catholic school. They were as smart as me. They had no semblance of care about how they were taught or what they learned being better or worse than what I did in school. In short, as children, we did not put an emphasis on such things as a better education.

Such thoughts surrounding our education today, are in dire need of accountability. The salary structure for public school teachers is quite reasonably considered good. The salary structure for catholic school teachers – where as much as $6000.00 or more is required tuition for each student is considerably lower than that of the public school teachers.

In a place where parents pay for education, the teachers make less. While the schools that provide free education make more money. Is there something wrong with this picture? The Catholic community as a whole has gone through a transition in the 21st century. The scandals related to priest abusing children is a worldwide travesty. This has not made a difference with regard to cost when sending children to schools. In many ways it has made catholic education more expensive. Schools in and around the neighborhood I grew up in have been closed.

The theory around these closures, in my opinion are suspect.
The Church will give the story about diminished enrollments
in the neighborhoods where schools have been closed. The
truth, and something as Catholics we are not allowed to
discuss, has more to do with accountability. The real estate
many of the closed schools inhabit, in my theory is worth
more than the money to be made educating students. In part,
the scandals associated with massive worldwide ongoing
investigations has made even the proliferation of educating
children no longer profitable.

Accountability is the highest form of integrity available to us
as individuals. When our governments can make accusations
against one another based entirely on envy, jealously and
hypocrisy – accountability is put at risk. When our hospitals,
pharmaceutical companies and the entire hierarchy of the
health care industry can slice and dice our care based on
monetary rewards – accountability is no longer valid. When
our schools and educational facilities can mandate how we
learn, what we learn and how we pay for it – accountability is
a joke.

Chapter 24

Barking up the Wrong Tree

It occurs to me now in my 60s, that we have a choice to look at our life experiences in two ways. We can choose to embrace what we learned and sense we gained a perspective that borders on wisdom; or we can feel and be thought of as naïve.

Since 2016, and what is being labeled as America's biggest challenge, there's something about the way information is processed and knowledge is shared that no longer seems to add up. We were always taught that "knowledge is power" when I was growing up. However, when did knowledge start becoming a detriment to how we view our own history?

The attention in today's world put on politics in every facet of our waking day has turned too many people against one another. The old adage that we should never mention politics, religion and sex in mixed company has somehow become something no one can practice without being thought of as ignorant.

What if, not caring about politics or what religion someone practices or who someone wishes to have sex with doesn't matter? What if, there were more people wishing politicians handled our country's needs without stepping one another's toes? What if, no one really cared what religion another person embraced? What if, who we chose to sleep with had nothing to with whether we could be happy or sad? What if, it didn't matter what color someone's skin might be?

Having lived now as I said into my 60s, I honestly believe these things do not matter. They matter only to individuals who hunger for attention in a crowded room. Whether or not you like how any politician is doing his or her job adds up to something else entirely. In the grand scheme of things, too many people want to feel they are championing a cause in the name of personal justice.

My friend Bill walked out of his front door on his 85th birthday, he fell and broke his hip. His whole life was turned upside down and inside out in a matter of seconds. He died six months later. My friend Tom did well for himself. He managed to retire at 55 years of age. Two years after retiring he was diagnosed with early on-set Alzheimer's.

I miss my two friends. We spent the past 30 years getting together to visit used book stores up and down the East Coast. Now I am helping to clean their homes of the books they loved. A monumental task considering they were collectors of history, philosophy and stories of America throughout time.

What will be found if no book stores remain; ten, twenty, thirty years from today? Will future generations look at our society as innovators or stagnations? Will they have reached a wisdom it appears fewer and fewer people have today?

There are thousands of quotes from reputable poets, writers, thinkers, singers, comedians, politicians and clergy members defining hatred. There are an equal number, if not more by similar groups defining love. It is considered courageous to lambast someone or something we dislike today; and it is often labeled sentimental drivel to endorse love has a universal appeal.

How and when did this happen? Those on one side of today's fences will argue it happened in 2016. In a manner of extreme naiveté, the issues that separate us as Americans has plagued us all long before a single election. The way we choose to take sides today is no longer an exhibit of rational behavior.

Some men see things as they are and ask why. Others dream things that never were and ask why not." - George Bernard Shaw

I believe many people are barking up the wrong tree. Newspapers, radio talk shows and television news channels are the equivalent to the one kid we all knew growing up. He or she was the one most likely to disagree with anyone over anything because it was fun to watch how upset they got. We are all subscribing to that one kid's philosophy today.

I have been alive through a dozen presidency's, (Eisenhower, JFK, Lyndon B Johnson, Nixon, Ford, Carter, Reagan, Bush Sr., Clinton, Bush, Obama and Trump) and not one has changed how I or anyone I know live their daily lives.

Milk and bread gets delivered to the supermarket the same way it always did long before any of these presidents took office. Advancements in how we accept one another is the biggest and most recognizable accomplishment of the past 100 years here in America.

And yet, we refuse to embrace our accomplishments as a unified and dignified society. Instead, we react to incidents of hatred with vengeance. Most people of every race, religion and ethnicity alive today living in America will agree we have made strides in tolerance. However, there appears to be a divide amongst us that rips at the very foundation of our country's ability to learn from our mistakes.

There is an innate ability too many people hold on to like it was the meaning of life for them. This leads to the confusion and the controversies surrounding what and how we hear certain things discussed and envisioned today. We have in some ways become victims of our vicarious nature. We live through the words and actions of people we allow to influence us. Entertainers, newscasters, journalist who for reasons that cannot be fully understood share insights from one side of the aisle.

If a large group of people become convinced that what was said and done is against anything they firmly believe; we are all similar to the hate groups who hung innocent people because of the color of their skin. We are the same as dictators who kill because they hate people of a certain religion. Hatred has a history that knows no end if we continue to embrace our differences instead of acknowledging our similarities.

Entire families have been torn apart over political and religious opinions. More have been separated due to a lack of tolerance for sexual choices and racial prejudices. How is it we can believe our opinions or the translation of what is said and done is better or worse? It's a contradiction of human intelligence.

When entertainer's voce opinions like comparing Trump to Hitler, they are in serious need of psychological help. If we take a step back from such insane statements; we must try to comprehend what would make anyone make such a claim. For obvious reasons, Hitler was one of the worse tyrants of modern times. He was not only tyrannical, but delusional in more ways than can be fathomed by any rationale human being. He was responsible for the deaths of millions of innocent people. The comparison is not only proof of a person's lack of intelligence, it borders on being treason.

How far have we gone with regard to having people who say such things taken to task?

 Such accusations get the entertainer the craving for attention he / she needs to live. The more sensationalized any claim, the more likely it will find an audience. When people claimed they would leave the country if Trump got elected in 2016; they were catering to a quirky need for attention that in every instance had them staying put in America. I dare say what will these same morons do when he is elected again?

No one alive now or ever in the history of man likes War. The 1960s generation of which I am often reminded was my generation, is credited with starting a revolution. The revolution they embarked on changed the world for the better in many ways. However, there are elements of the same generation having endorsed a mindset that has through the years turned excellent changes in to crusades. The crusade was and remains conceptual at best.

Make Love Not War

The slogans of the 1960s had redeeming qualities. The practicality of expressing our want for "Peace on Earth" has universal appeal. However, there has never been a time in the history of the world when war was not a factor in separating husbands from wives, children from families, and countries torn asunder.

Turn on, tune in, drop out.
Timothy Leary

If history has taught us anything, the one constant has been "everything you hear and see may not be what it sounds or looks like. What has changed here in the 21st century is the new ability to read in to what we hear and see.

Those reading in to off the cuff commentary and rhetoric end up reacting in ways that further separates the truth from fiction.

The point of this book is simply this; we can choose to get along with one another or we can perpetuate stupidity on a grand scale. Timothy Leary endorsed the use of LSD in the 1960s. His quote "Turn, tune in, drop out" became a slogan for those individuals wanting to escape the world around them. Ironically, it could be said our use and reliance on information and how we get it today is our LSD.

We react like crazed lunatics on acid because something we read on social media. We react like puppets awaiting our strings to be pulled by news channels, papers and magazines run like separate camps in a tug-a-war. Twelve Presidents have not changed the one thing we all share as a nation. Love or hate is an option. We can continue to thrash away like a bunch of extras in an episode of the Game of Thrones – or – we can give peace a chance. This doesn't sound like a feasible possibility to many people, they want their cake and they want to eat it too.

Utopia is a concept like no other promised mental state available during the 1960s or the discussions of legalizing marijuana today in all 50 states. For those who need a stimulant to believe the world is a better place while under the influence of something - Rock On. In reality, things change for the better when we have open conversations without hatred as a motivating factor.

I heard a patient in the hospital where my friend Bill was recovering from his hip injury saying, "You know there's a cure for cancer; the bastards won't let us have it because the unemployment rate would be off the charts." There are several ways to translate someone's view of such a thing. One way is to denounce them as being delusional and suffering from dementia.

Another way would be to define such a person as cynical beyond reproach. And then there is a way to see this individual as hopeful despite his lack of faith in the medical industry.

Taking it one step further, this individual can be said to be a lot like many today; who embrace the utopian concepts of "make love, not war," but sadly only want peace on their terms. Personally, I wish my friend Bill was still alive. He passed away six months after entering a rehab center. I want my friend Tom to remember everything and everyone. I want us all to be happy.

Chapter 25

Sexual Identity as a Course in Madness

One of the oddest ways to stipulate how insane our world is today; has a lot to do with how individuals can now identify themselves. No longer is it appropriate to define oneself as male or female. There are movements in place throughout America to help parents identify the sex of their child at birth. The choices no longer represent the obvious distinction of boy or girl. Parents, have the option of simply identifying their child as "other." What may or may not fit into some progressive idealism based on what a person is – requires a need to be cognizant that a new born baby is what he or she is when delivered in to this world. The idea that parents do not want to label their children at birth, because it may impair their ability to choose who and what they want to be later in life – is a tad nuts to me. Or, am I being politically incorrect by using "nuts" in a statement about sexual identity?

The current list of possible sexual identities, according to websites galore on the Internet stands at 72 different variations related to how a person can self-define their sexual identity. Not that there's anything wrong with that…

The lists range from homo sapiens to various kinds of homosexuals.

Homo sapiens:

the primate species to which modern humans belong; humans regarded as a species.

Within the framework of our being human beings, which I believe many of us still are -- the most acceptable definition has been in existence for *more than 2 million years into the past until sometime between* **40,000 and 10,000 years ago** *(depending on who you ask).*

The manner in which some identities are defined can be amusing at times. The above italicized identity appears when typing in the phrase, "What is a caveman?" Given the only known explanation for what the first men and women were called – I took the liberty of identifying homo sapiens under the longest standing definition available. Unbeknownst to most people is a little known fact related to the existence of gay cavemen.

'Gay Caveman' Found by Archaeologists Near **Prague.** *A team of Czech archaeologists claim to have unearthed the remains of an early gay man from around* **2900-2500 B.C.** *outside Prague. According to the Telegraph, the "gay caveman" was found buried in a way normally reserved only for women during the Copper Age.*

Given this information, we can now safely assume that mankind has had homosexual alliances since the dawn of time.

Homosexuality:
the quality or characteristic of being sexually attracted solely to people of one's own sex.

The current means of sexual identity excludes the notion that any one person is attracted to partners of the same sex. The overall impression is that a person can now be attracted to different ways of identifying themselves. This is not as confusing as it sounds.

It is also something that given the evolution of mankind to be more aware of oneself, many people today do not wish to be categorized in any way that fits in to any acceptable stereotype.

Under the auspicious discovery of "diversity" as a guideline for respecting one's race and sexuality; several studies have been conducted in recent years to help people identify where they feel they fit in to society. A British city council out of Brighton and Hove, England distributed a gender survey to secondary school students in 2016.

The students were asked to check off from the below list all of the categories they felt associated with when identifying their sexuality.

- Agender

- All genders

- Androgynous

- Bi-gender

- Boy

- Demi-boy

- Demi-girl

- Female

- Gender fluid

- Gender nonconforming

- Genderqueer

- Girl

- In the middle of boy and girl

- Intersex

- Male

- Non-binary

- Not sure

The list was given to students who were at the time of the survey between the ages of 13 – 18 years of age. In response to the above criteria, several psychologist and sociologist voiced their condemnation of such forced categorization.

Come on folks, this is getting a bit ridiculous. Most middle-school and even college kids have trouble choosing between the many different flavors of ice cream at Baskin and Robbins, why force them to identify between genders and sexual orientations that they don't even understand!
Jeff Dunetz - at The Lid (which is defined as comments from the standpoint of a politically conservative, observant Jew.)

This kind of survey only scratches the surface when attempting to place individuals by their sexual identities in to any demographic.

So as to drive home the notion of our being, I share with you a list that falls under the following definition: *While sexuality is a spectrum and not a single filled bubble answer, there are two categories that divide human sexuality: monosexual and plurisexual. Within those two categories are 9 sexual orientations that have been given the abbreviation LGBQDPAK (Lesbian, Gay, Bisexual, Queer, Demisexual, Pansexual, Asexual, and Kink).*

Asexuality – are defined as people with no attraction to others.

Demisexuality – are individuals who have a deep emotional attraction to others. These individuals are often asexual with thoughts of desire towards others.

Heterosexuality – make up 96% of the United States population. The vast majority of the population are attracted to the opposite sex.

Androsexuality – are men attracted to all things male. They do not necessarily consider themselves hetero or homosexual.

Gynesexuality – are females attracted to all things female. They do not necessarily consider themselves hetero or homosexual.

Homosexuality – individuals attracted to same sex partners. For the sake of being politically correct, females are called lesbians and men are called gay.

Bisexuality – are men and women attracted to both genders.

Pansexuality - are sexually attracted to all other individuals, including males, females, or those who identify as anywhere in between.

Queer – is a rather old-school identity. It can be considered a derogatory word or be accepted by the gay / lesbian community as a form of one's sexuality.

Kink – are those people who relate to sex with regard to fantasies. The fantasies are related to different kinds of stimulation and practices.

Drs. Alfred Kinsey, Wardell Pomeroy, and Clyde Martin developed the Kinsey Scale in 1948 as a means of emphasizing that people generally fall on a spectrum, rather than identifying as exclusively as one sexual orientation.

*Note: The above information was collected when typing in the phrase what are the list of sexual identities. For further research on how much is available when attempting to identify sexuality, it is easily concluded you as a reader would not leave your home for the next 200 years.

The point of this chapter, is to illustrate the convoluted and highly confusing ways sexual identity is when trying to identify what each variance represents and means. The idea that parents, no matter how progressive they may wish to define themselves can interfere with a child's identity at birth – before a child can distinguish basic skills like talking – walking and understanding life's most challenging day-to-day experiences is not just insane: it is a form of abuse on par with punishing them for not being exactly what their parents want them to become.

In no way, does this chapter denigrate or insinuate that any person doesn't have the right to identify themselves sexually in any way they _naturally_ feel suits them. It is proof that progressive parenting borders on stupidity.

Chapter 26

Future Fears

Throughout this book, the different ways many in our society in the 21st century act and carry on every day, is undeniably irrational. The influx of exposure to everything around us, makes for a confusing future. While the advent of the Internet, may have been intended to provide us with a ways and means to better understand one another; it has served to cause more separation than anyone thought possible.

On any given day, comments from every avenue of society further denies us any semblance of what is in our best interest. Too much information denigrates our ability to ascertain reality from fantasy. Too much interaction within the worlds of fantasy erases any concept of reality.

For many years, there have been discussions about the effects of gaming.

Gaming:

>the action or practice of playing gambling games.
>the action or practice of playing video games.

The billion dollar industries surrounding the proliferation of "gaming" which can be tied to "On-Line Gambling" or the playing of video games continues to grow. Gambling, as a practice has been labeled an addiction for many years. The addiction related to video games is still in its infancy.

The World Health Organization added "gaming disorder" to its list of diseases. The disorder was NOT added to the American Psychiatry Association's manual, the DSM-5. This is alarming on many levels when discussing how such activities effects each person.

*The DSM-5 is **the Diagnostic and Statistical Manual of Mental Disorders**. This product is representative of more than 10 years of effort by hundreds of international experts in all aspects of mental health. Their dedication and hard work have yielded an authoritative volume that defines and classifies mental disorders in order to improve diagnoses, treatment, and research.*

The origins of the DSM date back to 1840 — when the government wanted to collect data on mental illness. The term "idiocy/insanity" appeared in that year's census.

Forty years later, the census expanded to feature these seven categories: "<u>mania</u>, melancholia, monomania, paresis, dementia, dipsomania and epilepsy."

But there was still a need to gather uniform stats across mental hospitals. In 1917, the Bureau of the Census embraced a publication called the *Statistical Manual for the Use of Institutions for the Insane.* It was created by the Committee on Statistics of the American Medico-Psychological Association (now the American Psychiatric Association) and the National Commission on Mental Hygiene. The committees separated mental illness into 22 groups. The manual went through 10 editions until 1942. *

*Source of reference – Wikipedia

- DSM-1 – was published in 1952 with a comprehensive listing of 106 disorders.

- DSM-2 – was released in 1968 with a listing of 182 disorders.

- DSM-3 – was released in 1987 included anxiety disorders and mood changes leading to schizophrenia. It listed 265 different disorders.

   An updated DSM-3 detailed 292 disorders.
- DSM-4 – released in 1994 listed 297 specific disorders.

- DSM-5 – released in 2013 consisted of 20 disorder oriented chapters proclaiming 300 kinds of disorders.

The increased levels of how the American Psychiatric industry has determined since 1952, our growing number of disorders fits in to this books intentions. Do the different number of disorders represent our having gone more crazy since 1952? Or, can it be said – the abilities of the Psychiatric industry to better understand us as a species best defines their analysis of us all?

I opt to take a neutral stand on this issue. In one way, it clearly stipulates my belief we are more crazy in the 21st century than we were in the 1950s. However, it cannot be disputed that here in the 21st century, our ability to get more and receive more stimulation has increased our innate capabilities for entitlement.

Is the average human being more susceptible to disorders based on the modernization of our everyday health? This is the basis of widespread questions related to our daily interactions and reactions to life itself.

As we proceed in to the future, how many different ways can we be analyzed? Can we now assume the increasing methods for better understanding one another can only become more diverse and filled with an almost infinite number of ways one person differs from another?

Will there be a time in our future when the disorders, like our DNA are subjected to everyone being different based on inherited traits? Some may argue, that disorders and traits cannot be compared. These people will suggest that our DNA is related to our genetic information in our bodies, while disorders are merely psychological. I would disagree.

As we proceed in to the 21st century, I personally see more and more diversity creating a norm that does not recognize individuality. In contrast to each person having their own genetic signature; psychiatrists are slowly proving we as a species can no longer evolve.

This theory deserves qualification. When in the company of different groups of people today – albeit members of any racial denomination or religious affiliation; I see similarities that constitute they lack individuality.

For example, a group of people declaring themselves as hipsters – inevitably seek to look and dress alike. Members of a certain sexual identity will over the course of time attain a look in public that provides them a sense of being accepted by others of their own circle.

Is this a disorder or a declaration of acceptable behavior? If psychiatrists are still uncovering the ways we act mentally, how long will it take for them to reach definitions for how we look physically, interact emotionally and sexually?

Is it only a matter of time before every human being,
according to the Psychiatric industry fall in to an acceptable
category, demographic or be defined as someone with a
disorder?

What influences our disorders? If how we look and dress can
be used a ways and means to immediately define us, is
fashion a disorder?

If we act and say things when in the company of people who
do not subscribe to our understanding, is media a disorder?

I'm Nobody! Who are You?

Emily Dickinson (poet)

I'm nobody! Who are you?
Are you nobody, too?
Then there's a pair of us -don't tell!
They'd banish us, you know.

Chapter 27

Entitlement

On January 31st, 2020, two very significant events took place. In Great Britain – a vote that took place in 2016 was finally acknowledged. Great Britain had posed the idea of leaving the European Union, of which it was a member for over 45 years. By leaving the EU, several key factors will inevitably occur in the years to come. Some believe, the decision will send the nation into chaos. Others embrace the idea as a form of independence, where by Great Britain will control its own future without allegiance to any trade regulations or restrictions mandated by a larger unified group.

On the same day, a vote was taken at the trial for impeaching Donald Trump as President of the United States. The vote passed by a narrow margin (51-49) in the Senate to stop any need for more witnesses, brought about different takes on whether justice had been served.

On the front pages of the NY Daily News and N.Y. Post, the headlines payed homage to a fallen basketball star – Kobe Bryant, who along with his daughter and 7 other people died in a helicopter crash on January 26, 2020. The overall coverage of this horrible tragedy was and is more important than any need to embellish the nonsensical need for governments to carry out its all-encompassing rhetoric about something both Great Britain and the United States need to desperately get past.

This of course, will be disputed by individuals who have since 2016 become obsessed with their hatred and disdain for things happening in the world that are not to their liking.

If a study could be made based on the prior chapter's increasingly list of disorders; one can make the case that many people today suffer from a sense of entitlement, more so than ever before in human history.

It is this one form of human behavior that makes so many in our society disgruntled, bitter, vindictive and filled with hatred. So many men and women carry around with them problems associated with "what might have been," instead of embracing the concept of "what is."
In an effort to share these insights, I sent the following letter to a local newspaper:

<u>New Year Brings Undue Pressure</u>

It is quite interesting to witness our annual want for new beginnings. Every New Year brings with it a sense of renewal.

We are all prone to making resolutions of some kind. Whether we consciously or subconsciously react to the need for bettering ourselves, the constant reminders of sticking to a better diet or a need to exercise fills the airwaves and takes up countless pages in newspapers.

The annual evolutionary process of how well each person does when addressing these motives for improvement is quite fascinating.

While everyone can gain a better overall experience regarding advantages to our health and well-being when pursuing better life practices, there's also the possibility of these positive motives becoming negative elements.

When witnessing the annual commitment made every year by friends and relatives, I am often reminded of more people being exhausted and disappointed come February.

A study should be done as to how many people become frustrated with the demands they have placed on themselves through the month of January.

The discipline required for sustaining good health is not always about a good diet and daily exercise. It's been my experience that another important aspect to sustainable good health is attitude.

By February, the average person becomes affected by expectations. Promises made from infomercials guaranteeing weight loss in a projected time period mixed with every person's want to succeed causes a sense of failure.

This is not a realistic failure related to lifelong accomplishments or achievements. However, our innate want to feel and look better cannot be measured without our wanting to see good results.

I don't believe anyone has a better handle on remaining healthy. It is my feeling that each person is responsible for their own well-being. The only proven practice I can believe in; is maintaining a healthy attitude.

Still, here too, the overall experience of trying to stay positive can be exhausting. We are surrounded by negativity today.

We can wake up feeling fully refreshed and ready to take on the world, only to turn on the radio, television or check our social media sites and become overwhelmed by what we find.

In a song from years ago, "Spanish Pipe Dream," songwriter John Prine suggests "Blow up your TV, throw away your paper/Go to the country, build you a home/Plant a little garden, eat a lot of peaches/Try an' find Jesus on your own."

The suggestions may seem rather outdated or perhaps too New Aged for many of us today, but the sentiment is valid and timeless.

It does not mean to literally blow up your television. The suggestion is merely good advice to turn it off when what's happening is too upsetting. The remainder of the lyrics can help everyone when dealing with our daily stress.

As 2020 gets into high gear, which translates into our daily routines, perhaps we can benefit from not placing pressure on ourselves and one another. Everything is not always about what we believe we can control and how we want things to be.

The Rolling Stones taught us years ago that "You can't always get what you want, but if you try, sometimes you get what you need."

The point and relevance of my suggestion in this letter is that "attitude" is our key ingredient for finding any semblance of national and universal balance. Sadly, this mindset is lost on individuals who defend their ignorance as a form of rational thought.

The studies in place related to our everyday actions, related to what we eat, how we eat and who we eat with, not to mention what we watch, how we choose to watch it goes to prove our daily lives are on trial. If we do not fit into a demographic or category that can be easily monitored and therefore criticized, we are considered outsiders.

Being labeled an outsider is the biggest crime we can exhibit on the global stage. Not wishing to abide by a mindset that fosters inclusiveness over individuality makes any outsider appear unhinged and unwelcomed. The very worst of us, as outsiders, are those still willing to think for ourselves.

When speaking with the younger generations today, I am fascinated by terms they freely express as their defense against logic and free thought.

Terms like "cancel culture" and "woke" leak in to their conversations depicting a sense of entitlement over that of respecting another's opinion or way of life different than their own. The hypocrisy of these cultural devices or attitudes – defies logic while being conceived as a unifying thought process. Very intelligent and highly educated men and women are incapable of seeing how irrational they act and sound.

It is akin to a bully in a schoolyard being the one kid the students most fear so they follow his / her every lead. While thinking themselves revolutionary because they all want to be on the same page, they inadvertently lose any regard for their own thoughts.

Cancel Culture - A variant of the term, cancel culture, describes **a form of boycott** in which someone (usually a celebrity) who has shared a questionable or unpopular opinion on social media is "cancelled."

Woke - being aware, and "knowing what's going on in the community."

In both of these terms, the most relevant definition has more to do with anyone not fitting into the mindset of the people declaring another person dismissed or unwelcomed. It takes years, in many cases a lifetime for one person – no less any group of people to experience positive change in their lives.

It defies common sense to dismiss anyone because they do not subscribe to a single mindset. Today, the opposite is true in every aspect of daily living.

"Interpretations of interpretations interpreted."
— **James Joyce**

As a society, we now communicate with the written word more often than actually having conversations. We interpret what is meant and rarely fully understand what is actually being said.

"Nothing said in words ever came out quite even. Things in words got twisted and ran together, instead of staying straight and fitting together."
— **Ursula K. Le Guin**

When a society relies only on what is written, abbreviated in to sentences related to a given event or act, we risk losing our ability to understand each other, no less what actually happened. This is the rabbit hole we have fallen in to on so many topics and ideas. To continue digging in the same hole will only leave us more separated and lost. If everyone feels they are entitled to the same things, they lose sight of what it took for others to get what they own. Entitlement, like socialism is a false representation of equality for all.

What each person feels they deserve is subject to change when some get it and others do not. If you lose weight on a diet doing the same things another does who doesn't lose weight – you're no longer praised, you're considered cancelled. If you like someone or something who's been cancelled, you're labeled a fool. This is our modern world. Only woke individuals need apply.

<u>**Socialism**</u>

any of various economic and political theories advocating collective or governmental ownership and administration of the means of production and distribution of goods.

a system of society or group living in which there is no private property.

a system or condition of society in which the means of production are owned and controlled by the state.

It would take me several lifetimes to comprehend why any of our fellow Americans would find this acceptable. And yet, there is a youth oriented movement today who embrace the concept as part of their disillusioned sense of equality for all.

It is quite fashionable today to imagine a world filled with peace and tranquility for everyone. The basis of this thought process has many advocates. They often quote John Lennon's song "Imagine" as their anthem or reasoning for this utopian mindset.

What is quite comical about this thought process is the underlining hypocrisy of its premise. While I myself am a huge Beatles and John Lennon fan, I can't subscribe to a mindset that comes from an artist dreaming out loud with a guitar. As someone who considers music to be our most cherished creation by mankind, I can't give over my brain cells to something that makes my body move joyfully.

Attempting to understand why millennials like the idea of socialism over that of capitalism is difficult to explain – but so easy to understand. A vast majority of the younger generation has yet to make enough money or spend enough time working for a living. They are duped into believing the world would be a better place if every day expenses were paid for by others or in most cases government subsidized programs. What is easily lost in this belief is how much of their income is needed to make these programs functional. The BIG PICTURE mandates that here in America nothing is free and you get what you pay for in life.

According to a HUFFPOST *article - With a more liberal outlook on social issues, Millennials are re-defining the word socialism, equating it with a "gentler" way of life, while maintaining the American value of working hard to get ahead. Taking care of each other, while enjoying the life we've been given. They've not given up on the theory that everyone should work to get ahead, but believe there is a better way that will benefit the working class as much as the corporations and uber rich have been benefitted.*

As is the case with many Internet-driven blogs and commentary, a slant is made to appease the mindset of those people who subscribe to the rants. The same article goes on to champion the millennials want for a better society. The overall concept of living a more "gentler" way of life plays in to the manner in which most millennials grew up.

During every phase of their lives, awards were given to most for being participants in any endeavor they pursued. In Sports and in every facet of their educational pursuits; trophies and accolades were given to most without repercussions associated with learning to be gracious losers or sub-par students.

The bar has been set so far below the standards expected of prior generations, the only blame for how they view the world can be placed on us for allowing them to become so mislead.

Now, as they have reached an age of responsibility, when the transition in to the real world is at hand for them – they opt to embrace the same mindset that gave them kudos for doing less than was necessary to get by. Now, as they become voters, they wish to endorse candidates who make promises that have no basis in reality.

The scary part about the whole ordeal is how far reaching the promises of more for doing less today. The entitlement factor rises its ugly head again.

Chapter 28

American Hurt

Our world is filled with double standards and contradictions. In 2019, a book was published which has taken on an entirely new life based on how it is being perceived. The book, "American Dirt" by Jeanine Cummins was endorsed by the Oprah Winfrey Book Club and is quickly making its way on to best seller list. The hilarity of the condemnation of this book makes for a perfect example with regard to our being profoundly insane.

I confess to not having read the book. I did see a huge display of the book in a major bookstore. I glanced through the opening pages to see if I liked the writers style of writing. I admit it was not being to my liking. However, I do take offense to how the book is experiencing controversy and support the writer's right to publish her story.

I can associate with the overall experience of the book, a novel, being questioned by people. When I released my novel, "Something in the Neighborhood of Real," I was thrilled to have it reviewed and labeled worthy of a book signing at a major book store. The experience was something that made me proud. Leading up to the reviews and subsequent sales of the book, I was often amused by the questions received from newspapers and readers.

The New York Daily News ran a full page review of the novel. In the review they quoted my childhood friend, Tom Huber,

who a character in the book was based upon. They asked him if events in the book were true.
The comical nature of this question, to this day makes for an explanation related to how we as a society read. The definition of a novel is necessary so as to fully explain the significance of how stark raving mad we have become.

Novel
a _**fictitious prose narrative**_ of book length, typically representing character and action with some degree of realism.

I allude to the definition in defense of how fiction is different from non-fiction. The inability to substantiate a difference gives credibility to how many in our society today lack the ability to read anything. Instead, we **read in to** everything, with a wanting desire to prove the text of books illegitimate or false narratives about the world we want to live in.

While my book cannot be compared to the success of any best seller, I can understand how bizarre and quite literally ridiculous it is for me to feel a need to mention American Dirt as an example of our world's stupidity.

The argument being discussed, and given credence by the media has to do with the subject matter of the book not being written by someone who could understand the plight of her own characters. The premise of the book has to do with Mexican immigration and how one family experiences hardships and challenges. There are people complaining the author, who is not Mexican could never know the experience of what she describes in the book. Some have gone so far as to say the author is exploiting Mexican immigrants and their plight to live decent lives and ultimately seek admission in to the United States.

The lunacy of this argument is on par with our needing to accept that any author who has ever written a book about his / her characters having gone in to space has to be an astronaut. It is further denigrated by the fact that novels are written with a semblance of imaginative episodes and chapters which have no basis of being considered realistic.

Notwithstanding, this simplistic definition can be easily disputed by some based on the above mentioned description of what constitutes a novel –
"typically representing character and action with some degree of realism."

It can be argued that we have lost the ability to read anything without it having to do with something / anything defined as real. It is very amusing for me to discuss this in any way given the title of my own novel. And yet, when we as a society watch reality TV with the same interest we may watch a scripted situation comedy; much can be understood how so many today; can no longer understand there's a difference between what is real and what is imagined.

The massive success of many books in recent years can be used as an example to prove my point. The success of the HBO series "The Game of Thrones" was based on a book series by George R. R. Martin. The phenomenon of the HBO series created a sensation that crossed over into the fashion and home décor industries. The same can be said of the Harry Potter books by J. K. Rowling. Both of these authors have gone on to be considered _**Gods**_ in literary circles. To achieve this status, a writer has to be the author of a book or series of books that reaches cult status.

Once attaining this status, the books take on a life larger than life itself. Both of the above mentioned series went on to become films (Harry Potter) and series (Game of Thrones) with massive appeal. Postal Carriers around the world were told to deliver Harry Potter books as if they were carrying the keys to a kingdom. Millions of fans around the world stood on lines for hours to take pictures of themselves sitting on the Iron Throne.

A genre of writing, read for pure escapism is the biggest selling attribute sort after by the publishing industry. Without it, controversy makes for the next best thing. While I am championing the right of any author to publish their story whether or not they were an astronaut; the Publishing industry is no doubt salivating over the free publicity given the book American Dirt.

The hurt factor has more to do with how far we have fallen from seeing things for what they really are today. It depicts a society's reaction to something so miniscule and ridiculous being used as a means to create widespread interest. It makes me wish now I wrote my novel using characters from another planet.

Chapter 29

The Molestation of Protest

First Amendment to the Constitution
Congress shall make no law respecting an establishment of religion, or prohibiting the free exercise thereof; or abridging the freedom of speech, or of the press; **or the right of the people peaceably to assemble**, *and to petition the Government for a redress of grievances.*

The directive established by the Constitution affords all citizens certain inalienable rights. Whether or not we can agree on what – where or when people exhibit their rights is a bone of contention in modern America. The decision of any person to protest with regard to something / anything they do not agree with is many times lost in translation.

The ongoing and most prolific form of protest in America today has much to do about nothing. I make this claim half-heartedly based on my absolute disdain for anyone who would disrespect the National Anthem or our American flag. Similar to the misunderstood reasons for embracing socialism, I believe many who have a dislike of anything here in America does not afford them the right to publicly disgrace our adopted symbols of unity.

I would venture that those people displaying such acts of disrespect are often seeking attention for themselves more so than being serious about anything they say is there reason for such appalling displays. In my view, if the events or actions which they proclaim to be so disturbing they have to publicly display themselves as "martyrs for a cause" – there are any number of better ways to make a difference.

The most alarming nature of recent displays of disrespect come from established athletes and performers who are first and foremost exhibiting a hypocrisy beyond any definition of concern for the greater good. The acts of rebellion are formulated in ways to put the spotlight on themselves – and most times end up clouding the storylines behind their protest.

In America, the many different examples of every day equality are visible in ways that cannot be measured. On city blocks throughout every state in the nation, a multitude of different cultures and ethnicities live without incident. Granted, there is not always a harmony related to everyone getting along; however, for the most part very few neighborhoods live within the framework of hatred proposed by acts of protesting the American way of life.

Where there are individuals who would terrorize a neighborhood in to seeking curfews or fear for their children; a much larger concern should be in the bright lights of any protest. The individuals who feel they can denigrate our shared symbols of Democracy should realize that negative displays of unity lead to chaos and mayhem.

A more enlightened form of protest would be to display compassion for anyone harmed or in danger. The need for positive role models is lacking in America today. The very few reminders we receive with regard to real heroes is often dismissed. Soldiers, First Responders, Doctors, Nurses and Teachers deserve such recognition. Men and women who spend their days helping others instead of complaining should be hailed as heroes.

Heroes do not wear custom made jewelry that costs more than someone's car. Heroes do not get endorsements from billion dollar corporations because they are easily recognizable. The ignorance of such acts of stupidity displays an inability to know when they are being exploited. It further displays their insincerity about anything he / she wants to protest, because in the end, quite obviously, it's all about the money.

The same ways disenfranchised or lost souls can be recruited On Line or through different methods of enrollment by terrorist groups leads to the same kind of hateful influences and acts of regression. What feels to these protestors like a _stand_ against something or anyone ends up becoming a negative means to illustrate their own shortcomings.

Another highly evocative way of protest today has to do with people who get whimsical ideas. These ideas are without question so crazy they warrant dismissal by anyone with an ounce of intelligence.
Instead of being dismissed, they are embraced in the same way a group of people might get in on a high school prank.

In New York City on January 31, 2020 – a group of protestors impinged the use of the public subway system demanding "Transit is a Right." The group went so far as make demands that the NYPD be abolished. They wanted less police on the subways and they wanted to ride for free.
They called themselves *Decolonize This Place* – comprised of a left-wing coalition made up of some 30 separate groups. These types of acts and the development of such coalitions of protest are the direct result of how far reaching the disrespect displayed by athletes kneeling and performers and others sitting during the National Anthem.

What appears on the surface to be a rightful display afforded to everyone under the Constitution; is easily misread and in the end creates nothing except upheaval and acts of vandalism. At a time when safety of all people is paramount to securing our want for a better world, the molestation of protest as a false method of making a difference leads to dangers and worst acts of terror, placing us all in harm's way.

There are plenty of good reasons for fighting, but no good reason ever to hate without reservation, to imagine that God Almighty Himself hates with you, too.
Kurt Vonnegut

Chapter 30

Decorum and Disgrace

Decorum: *behavior in keeping with good taste and propriety.*

a particular requirement of good taste and propriety.

Disgrace: *loss of reputation or respect as the result of a dishonorable*

action bring shame or discredit on (someone or something).

During the 2020 State of the Union Address, President Donald J. Trump with the threat of being Impeached the very next day shared his view of the real America. Putting aside his own personal feelings of how he was viewed by individuals in Congress, he put forth to the American people his want for a better tomorrow.

At every juncture of the speech, the Speaker of the House, Nancy Pelosi – sitting behind him made faces and muttered to herself like a crazed lunatic. The obviousness of her hatred was at times distracting and culminated with her tearing the pages of the speech in two at the end. Throughout, the speech, snippets are seen of her tearing slices in to pages of the speech so as to make the grand gesture of dismissing everything she heard.

Also, during the speech – female members of the Democratic Party, sitting in uniformed white dresses and pant suits made certain they were noticed like a gang displaying their colors in a street fight. The lack of decorum and disgrace of actions as members representing the people of this country is highly appalling.

On February 5th, 2020, the day after the State of the Union Address, the U.S. Senate sat in the same room in Congress to vote on the Impeachment. The members of the U.S. Senate have been at war with one another since November 2019 when the House of Representatives charged the President with Obstruction of Congress and Abuse of Power. The results totally acquitted the President of both charges.

It would of course be crazy, given the current state of America, to celebrate the claim of acquittal without being totally aware of the partisan voting in the Senate. The Democratic Party is in many ways bewildered to accept any results without denigrating the process and the President.

Any American with an ounce of intelligence would be open to hearing logical evidence to support any claims of impeachable acts by the President. However, instead, with hatred as their only cry for justice, I implore the American people to stand up to such ignorance. I find myself writing this book in hopes it will stand as a ways and means to fully understand the truth.

When searching for an article on line the day after the results of the President's acquittal in the Senate – when typing in *Impeachment in the Senate Results;* there was very little to find. Instead, the vast majority of links on the day after this historic event, most articles available were about the charges of impeachment during the trial in the House of Representatives.

This is beyond my comprehension. It should unnerve anyone who believes in justice and truth as an American citizen.

A Republican senator, Mitt Romney crossed party lines to vote for impeachment. He proclaimed the decision as an act of conscience. It would make sense if he was not angered by the President not making him the Secretary of State in 2016. The acts of hatred and disdain were on display throughout the process to impeach the President.

Why has our country come to this manner of disgrace? It is to me both amusing and very telling of how far sore losers and opportunist will go and what they will do and say to maintain their own sense of credibility. Throughout this book I have offered examples that I hope prove beyond any doubt how separated America has become.

In my own family, much to my chagrin and disappointment I have witnessed how hatred leads to an embrace of blindness. I have heard excuses about the President's demeanor. His harsh declarations against people, places and things turning some individuals in to raving lunatics against anything he says and does. I have heard claims of him doing things that people argue disgusts them. I have sat in the company of family members so ill-informed they would rather alienate anyone who does not see the world through their eyes.

What I learned in my lifetime, is what I hope you dear reader learned as well. As rational and intelligent people, we cannot not follow such acts of disgraceful behavior. In every family, there are issues and experiences that divide the expectations and opinions of each person. Only respectful and open dialogue can create an atmosphere of understanding each individual's opinions. We must never show a lack of respect for someone merely because it is popular to do so.

What modern technology has done for the world is without question one of the major accomplishments in our unified history as human beings. It has allowed us the ability to communicate with each other. If we choose to meet and chat with people all over the world, we can do so from our computers and phones with the click of a button. Nothing has ever been more powerful and resourceful.

The capabilities are endless. They should offer us countless ways to embrace the world we all share. The sad reality is, we as a society do not deserve such a tool of communication. We cannot learn the very simple lesson of decorum. We humiliate ourselves when we choose to use such a luxury as a way of attacking others. Our future generations may one day find a way to respect one another with open dialogues and insightful ideas that better the world they live in.

Hopefully, in the future, family discussions can reach a balance once accorded the dignity of a respectable family dynamic. I respected my mother and father's generation despite their having been raised with different standards of living. I may have disagreed with their archaic mindsets related to religion and sexual freedoms, but I never acted out in such a way as to disrespect them.

I believe this point is essential for understanding the powers of the Internet. People having the ability to discuss anything today, lose the one necessary and vital tool for attaining any semblance of respect for each other – face-to-face real time conversations. Without the want or desire to step away from the safety net of like mindedness creates a society of stagnant individuals.

I fear the damage has been done for all of us today. My hope is that my grandchildren will find a way to accept one another based entirely on their want for a better world.
I pray they can discover a ways and means to embrace our differences without taking sides because it's fun or fashionable. I want to believe; they will know better than to feel any need for thinking themselves smarter or better than anyone. I wish for them a way out of the asylum they were born in to.

Chapter 31

Misnomers

Misnomer:

A wrong or inaccurate name or designation.

A wrong or inaccurate use of a name or term.

One of the biggest misnomers of the 21st century is the distinction of naming one another and others with titles we do not fit in to. The biggest misnomer of all is that of labeling Donald Trump a politician. This distinction has been branded on him because he became the President of the United States as the auspicious candidate for the Republican party. Many need to be reminded he never held a political office prior to his becoming the President. This is essential when attempting to understand the many ways he is disliked. It is imperative we as a nation also understand, his past does not coincide with the things he managed to get accomplished despite nothing but controversy and adversity throughout his years in office.

What needs to be further understood is how far reaching the opposition he has endured during his first term in office. By opposition, I am pointing out the differences of opinion and changes in how the government functions being at the core of what the Democratic party candidates claim to have a better

way of getting things done. This is by far the worst kind of strategy any one of the candidates can take.
It cannot be denied that in the first term of Trump's administration, the brazen disregard for protocols established over many years actually works.

The Democratic Party during the beginning stages of debates to establish the front runner for candidacy consist of men and women hell bent on winning over the populace – based entirely on which one hates President Trump the most. This kind of plan will only serve to further alienate the American people.

Yes, there are people who have the same level of disdain for how President Trump operates on a daily basis. The problem is, while they may oppose his methods, they relish in his success. The different mindsets that propose changes in how the country functions, albeit Socialism and idealisms associated with the Green New Deal – would take decades to implement and quite frankly include proposals that would not work here in America.

The hopeful elitist thought process related to beating Donald Trump is based on methods and concepts – his election in 2016 nullified and made void. The American people, without consciously realizing it – are now witness to a new world order. The politicians who governed the America of the 20th century can no longer become President of the United States.

This bold and agreed upon controversial proclamation needs to be accepted by many Americans. The failure of future elections and campaigns will only serve to disappoint anyone who still believes in the old school ways of Politicians rising through the ranks to become President. Governments are not like churches, where only those indoctrinated in to the regime can become leaders. The people do not cast votes so as to anoint anyone President. The President is not a religious leader like a Pope in the Catholic Church.

We have been exposed to an entirely different way of doing everything. His influence on the American psyche has been both enlightening and nauseating. According to polls related to his popularity in 2020, it is said America is split 50/50. This translates to 50% of the population accepting him as the President, and the 50% sadly following those who hate him down a rabbit hole.

This book has dealt with the many different areas I feel we have lost any connection to reality. On the political landscape, we have not just lost our minds, many people have gone totally insane. What was presented as an essay to explain my personal viewpoints related to where and when we traded common sense for lunacy is easily established when mentioning the disconnect related to politics.

The repudiation I wish to share has more to do with how we all need to get over ourselves. The indifferences established and inherited in our lifetime does not include hating one another for reasons associated with who is our President. As I mentioned in Chapter Four – *It's Always Temporary*. This mantra made by my 100-year-old mother-in-law should be our unified chant. Those people who embrace the ways President Trump conducts himself will have to one day realize this to be true based on the two-term limit of the office. The same cause for celebration will be rewarded to those who dislike him for the same reason. **It's Always Temporary.**

The concern then becomes, who will lead the country with the same dynamic force to be reckoned with on the world stage? Do voters want a figure head with a complacent manner of smiling for the cameras – or do we all need to stay vigilant and aware of how the world has changed in ways that warrant a leader who will not be fooled?

Epilogue

In closing, what some will label a manifesto, others will declare my claims to be nothing more than the ravings of a madman – I challenge you the reader to live a more positive life. I feel it is necessary to remind you again, I am not registered as a Republican or Democrat voter. *As an Independent voter, which I believe most people will be in the future – I have no affiliation with a party.* I have no allegiance to one political party being better than the other. I vote for who I believe will do the best for the America I love.

I don't wish to beat a dead horse by driving home the points made in this book. I will emphasize that above all indifferences I may have with family and friends about my political, religious and other topics of relevancy in a changing world, I respect their right to disagree with me. My one disappointment is having never received the same courtesy.

I can be proven wrong a million times during my life. The lessons learned in life from mistakes are my own to accept. I stand by my belief, that in any society, there is no room for hatred of anyone.

"Always remember, others may hate you, but those who hate you don't win unless you hate them, and then you destroy yourself."

Richard Nixon

One of the most important lessons in my lifetime has been what I am proudest of – keeping an open mind. Richard Nixon, who chose to resign rather than put the country through an Impeachment in the 1970s was my Commander in Chief when I served in the U.S. Army.
As a soldier, during a time of incredible unrest, I stood by him no matter how the media or public opinion swayed. As a soldier, I took an oath which demanded I respect America and follow the orders of the President. Every soldier today takes this same oath. To disgrace the oath in any way, to me, is a form of personal treason.

When my childhood friend Tom Huber chose to stand in front of a crowded auditorium at a Long Island, NY library giving a speech about Richard Nixon; I witnessed firsthand what an angry mob looks and sounds like. The room was filled with individuals who had entered the library with one thing in mind – to disrupt and insult my friend.

At the time Tom gave the speech, he stood with dignity and respect for the subject which he chose to discuss. The audience in my opinion acted like crazed idiots who in many ways are similar to the same people who exhibit the hatred for Donald Trump today.

Tom's speech was informative and respectful about the truth of our history. That same history that is being threatened today by people with one goal in mind – to distort the truth and hasten their want for being thought intelligent.

If they bothered to hear Tom's speech, they would have learned things about themselves many to this day are not willing to accept. The same kind of mentality being parlayed in to rallies and protest against a candidate simply because he doesn't placate their liberalist mindsets.

Tom, soon after giving the speech was diagnosed with *Early-on-set Alzheimer's*. If stress has any way of contributing to the horrid disease of Alzheimer's, I am convinced he gave his heart, mind and soul to defend someone he and I both respected.
My point, as this book comes to a close has all to do with how many in our nation today would choose to hate someone or anything based entirely on their unwillingness to communicate. I weigh in with what I see as our nation's biggest joke – that of having people more inclined to embrace agendas over facts. These very same people will undoubtedly come to believe that the Coronavirus originated in Corona, Queens.

I leave you with my theory about our being bat shit crazy to continue down any path filled with dissension and hatred of others. I leave you with my belief that racism is only real to those unwilling to accept the virtues and values of others. I leave you with the notion, no one who knows and appreciates love as the only way to make a difference has any right to demean who we choose to support.

And in the end, the love you take, is equal to the love you make.

The Beatles

Acknowledgements

This book would not be possible without the guidance of readily available articles and information found on the Internet for all of us to utilize. I suggest the Internet be used for the purpose it was created – to help mankind better ourselves and to assist us in staying informed while keeping an open mind. I warn you the reader, the Internet while full of information; is as dangerous as any dark alley after midnight. Lurking behind every discovery of knowledge are the same lies and deceptions we try to stay one step ahead of in our daily lives.

All information is shared without any laws as to how it can be interpreted. If something challenges your belief in trusting it is valid, pursue methods of getting the full story when speaking with someone in your family or a teacher you can trust. I acknowledge that the information I shared in this book is valid and trust worthy. I acknowledge that some things I shared may be met with scrutiny. I emphasize what I shared in the Prologue of this book – if it is not to your liking, write a book yourself to refute my claims.

Jonathan Kiddrane

2020

About the Cover Photos

The front cover photo was taken outside of an American Legion Hall in Upstate, NY. When I passed the hall, several thoughts crossed my mind. The first thought had to do with my not believing it was on display in such a way. My second thought was that of my feeling upset. Several years ago, when I moved in to my house, as the moving truck unloaded furniture and family belongings – I noticed an American flag being thrown away in a garbage can across the street. I asked a man standing in front of the house why he was throwing away the flag. "Who needs such a thing?" he yelled as I retrieved the flag from the trash. I took the flag and placed it on a holder in front of my new home. The man yelled, "Maybe it will give you better luck than it did me!" I have thought about that exchange many times over the years. I have watched how a flag can be viewed as a symbol of hope and pride. I have watched how a flag can be dismissed as nothing more than a rag. I have listened to arguments made by many in America that the flag represents a tyrannical past which they proclaim is no longer valid on the world stage. The front cover photo is a depiction of how these people see America and my reaction to being how I see these people to be insane.

About the Author

Jonathan Kiddrane is the name used for a main character in the novel "Something in the Neighborhood of Real" by Craig Schwab

This is the first book using this name in the real world.